GOIN' UPTOWN

MARQUETTE'S
MARCH TO MADNESS
AND RETURN TO THE
FINAL FOUR

JOSEPH DECLAN MORAN

Author of *You Can Call Me Al:*
The Colorful Journey of College Basketball's
Original Flower Child, Al McGuire

FOREWORD BY RICK MAJERUS

PRAIRIE OAK PRESS
BLACK EARTH, WISCONSIN

Library of Congress Control Number: 2003109827
ISBN: 1-879483-92-0

Project Manager: Michael Martin
Assistant Project Manager: Erika Reise
Editor: Jerry Minnich
Designer: Colin Harrington
Photos courtesy of Marquette University

Printed in the United States of America by McNaughton & Gunn.

08 07 06 05 04 03   6 5 4 3 2 1

Prairie Oak Press, a division of Trails Media Group, Inc.
P.O. Box 317 • Black Earth, WI 53515
(800) 236-8088 • e-mail: books@wistrails.com
www.trailsbooks.com

DEDICATION

This book is dedicated to the memory of my younger brother, Brendan Anthony Moran, who loved watching Marquette Basketball. Brendan attended a number of games at the Milwaukee Arena, Bradley Center, and the Allstate Arena (nee Rosemont Horizon) during his short time on this earth. The last game we saw together was on January 19, 2002, at the Allstate Arena, when Marquette defeated DePaul behind Dwyane Wade's 35 points. I will always treasure those Marquette Basketball memories with Brendan.

ACKNOWLEDGMENTS

There are many people who had a hand in the creation of this book. First and foremost is Rick Majerus, who was gracious and generous with his time in writing the book's foreword. His connection to all three Marquette Final Four teams since 1974 and to the late Coach Al McGuire, made him the ideal candidate to write the foreword for this book. A big thank-you to coach's office staff in Salt Lake City, including his secretary, Sara Johnson, Whitney Lindgren and Jessica Bagley for their patience and help during the process. A big thank you goes out to Rich Pannella, head women's basketball coach at Cardinal Stritch University in Milwaukee, for putting me in touch with Coach Majerus. My gratitude goes out to Marquette radio play-by-play announcer Steve "The Homer" True for his quotes and for allowing me airtime on his radio show and Marquette radio broadcasts over the years. A big thank-you to George Thompson for his cover quotes for the book and his constant encouragement. I am privileged to know him. Coach Hank Raymonds for taking the time to talk to me and provide his own special perspective on the history of Marquette basketball. A special thank-you to his wife, Jinny, for her generous hospitality whenever I have been a guest in the Raymonds' home. Lori Nickel and Todd Rosiak of the *Milwaukee*

Journal Sentinel were also very generous with their time and anecdotes about Marquette basketball BC (Before Crean) and AC (After Crean). John Dodds of Doddsonsports.com and Dodds on Sports, for supplying tapes, CDs, media guides, and publicity on his radio show throughout this entire process and for my first book, "You Can Call Me Al." To Marquette President Rev. Robert A. Wild, for taking the time to talk to me about Tom Crean and the team and providing his perspective on Marquette's NCAA run. To photographer *extraordinaire* "Uncle John" Baker for his unique perspective during the NCAA Tournament. To John Fedders for taking the time to talk to me about Coach McGuire. To Marquette SID John Farina for providing the great photography that appears in the book. Thank you Jim Ganzer (a.k.a. I.W.B.) for your background and perspective on recruiting and the basketball program. Many thanks to Jerry Minnich of Trails Media Group for his fine editing, and for publishing my first book. I will always be grateful. To Anita Matcha, Mike Martin, and the crew at Trails Media Group for giving me the opportunity to tell this story. A big thank-you goes out to my parents, Joseph and Mary Moran, and in-laws, Allan and Nancy Edwards, for their constant encouragement. My brother-in-law Kurt Edwards for his computer expertise in e-mailing the manuscript. The biggest thank-you of all goes to my wife, Kristen Janet, and my daughter, Erin Grace, who have given me the love, patience, and encouragement to follow this project through to completion. Without Kristen, I never would have been on a flight to New Orleans or found a room at the Hotel Monteleone. I love you bunches and bunches and bunches, Kristen Janet and Erin Grace. The two loves of my life.

Joseph Declan Moran

Summer, 2003

FOREWORD

By Rick Majerus, Men's Head Basketball Coach, University of Utah

I n 1977, Marquette hanged its hat on the Warriors. A group of guys, by and large, from an urban landscape who catapulted Marquette University onto the national scene.

They did it with a quirky blend of team play and stifling defense, under the direction of an individual, Al McGuire, who not only thought outside the box, but lived there as well.

Al McGuire's '77 Warriors were in some ways the antithesis of what the Jesuits had wanted the Marquette experience to be. These were guys to whom Ignatian discernment was as foreign to their lives as grass growing in front of their homes. Most of them came from neighborhoods where the arrest warrants were sent to "occupants" because everybody was under arrest.

The Maestro McGuire added the occasional Wisconsin suburbanite, such as Bill Neary and Jerry Homan, to his hoops orchestra.

Al always used to talk about taking the left or the right turn onto Capitol Drive with his motorcycle when deciding whether to come to practice or not. Thank God the motorcycle went left more often than not, because the team needed McGuire's direction and guidance, perhaps more so off the court than on it. This book by Joe Moran tries to bridge the gap from that turbulent time to one that is more genteel, more materialistic, and to a campus that is more pristine than any of the old Warriors could ever have hoped to imagine.

Tom Crean subscribes to the philosophy that defense does indeed win games. Shot selection and allocation are of paramount concern, and he, like McGuire, still places perhaps the greatest premium on recruiting a quarter century later.

The catalyst was Dwyane Wade, the man who would take them to a place in the basketball stratosphere heretofore unimagined by the old Warriors and new Golden Eagles alike. Wade is profiled, characterized, and a Crean creation not unlike what Butch Lee was to McGuire's march through the tournament madness.

This book does a great job of pointing out similarities as well as contrasts. It shows how divergent routes can lead to success given the promise of team above all else. However, that bus must be driven by a strong personality, and in that way Crean and McGuire gripped the steering wheel in similar fashion. They were dictatorial, authoritative, and yet savvy and streetwise enough to give their players space to operate both on and off the court.

Each placed an emphasis on receiving a quality education, but because today's academic standards are so much higher, Crean has received more pastoral guidance from the friendly Jesuit enclave on Wisconsin Avenue.

Coach Crean's student-athletes were more capable and better able to capitalize on the tremendous academic experience that is at the heart of what Marquette really has to offer, than those disparate "playschoolers" of an era past.

The chaplains on the bench may have differed. It used to be Father Piotrowski. Father Kelly led prayers for the Queen of Victory on this ride. Nevertheless, the insistence that you behave as a good person and adhere to the core principles of what Catholic education entails was a given in both eras. A genuine concern and compassion for other students is still evident in the conduct of the players, both on and off the court.

The formula for success remains one and the same, and Moran does a fabulous job of handling this parallel. I was fortunate to be the "go-to guy" for doughnuts, gas, cryptic correspondence to faculty and recruits alike, and even provided some of the players a driving lesson or two as I sat at the feet of two basketball giants, Al McGuire and Hank Raymonds.

In retrospect, these guys were the ideal "husband and wife" team. Al would kick their ass, even encouraged at the start of each game by the fans who enjoyed sending out a shout from above—"Give 'em hell, Al!" After the players were often severely reprimanded and egos were laid low, Hank Raymonds would put an arm around them and walk off into the night consoling or massaging the bruised psyches.

Coach Crean's temperament, singleness of purpose, energy, and effort very much parallels that of McGuire's. However, unlike McGuire, who had me on deck as a player confidant and aspiring coach, along with Raymonds as the consummate assistant coach, Crean has vamped with a posse of assistant coaches, one more capable than the next, to minister to the players' needs.

Similarities between Tom and Al are striking. Both are driven and committed, and loved to engage in inspiring and psychological ploys. Crean seems to find highly motivated and committed players who are able to run his many offensive sets. McGuire was a disciple of the K.I.S.S. Theory: Keep It Simple, Stupid, and believed in "Lombardian" execution.

Coach Crean is also a proponent of the fundamentals, but engages much more so in teaching them, unlike McGuire, because times have indeed changed. Coach Crean runs over 200 plays, to the wonderment of those from the '77 squad. Hell, there weren't even 200 trees on campus back in '77.

Crean seems to enjoy practice and embraces the day by looking forward to the start of it. Al enjoyed leaving practice, most of all, to go off with buddies like Jerry Savio and Joe DuChateau, former players like Brian Brunkhorst and Jack Burke, or paragons of the press like Curry Kirkpatrick and Pete Axthelm, and have a cocktail as he regaled them with the combative verbiage from that day's drills and scrimmage.

This book is a must-read for college basketball fans because it does a fine job of comparing and contrasting two coaches, both of whom overextended themselves as they reached for the Hoops Holy Grail at a relatively young age. And they did it with as different and distinctive coaching styles as you could imagine.

You will enjoy this trip taken into the basketball land that time forgot, as well as into the modern era which, in many ways, is all too antiseptic and unforgiving. It is a time and place where Al McGuire would be hard-pressed to be himself.

So, God speed to the Last Warrior and "Ring Out Ahoya" as Crean caroms off to another Final Four.

Salt Lake City, Utah
Summer, 2003

PROLOGUE:
SEASHELLS &
BALLOONS REVISITED

"We all had a taste of the honey [NCAA Tournament games, including 1974 Finals loss to North Carolina State]," remarked Maurice "Bo" Ellis before Marquette's 1976–77 championship season. "It was just a matter of getting it all together. Before the season we knew it was there. We knew what our goal was. Coach [McGuire] gave us a lot of confidence. Al kept everything under control. He had his players thinking what he wanted us to do. There was never a doubt about how good we were. It was just a matter of getting a few breaks. We had been there so many times, it was just a matter of getting over the hump."

Back in 1977, the last time a Marquette team made it all the way to the Final Four, the idea of "March Madness" had not yet been conceived by some young, hotshot sports producer on his way to the top of a network's sports division. Back then, there was no such thing as a three-point shot, a shot clock, or the alternate possession rule which all but eliminated the jump ball.

The 1976–77 edition of the Marquette Warriors started their tournament march as a long-shot underdog for the NCAA title, hoping to win it all for their retiring coach, Al McGuire. On Saturday afternoon, March 12, 1977, at the Omaha Civic Auditorium, the Warriors would play a grudge match against the University of Cincinnati. Fortunately, upon the team's arrival in Omaha, Al McGuire's "lucky" three-piece suit, which had been lost enroute, was found and the Warriors were ready to tangle with the Bearcats.

"That was not an easy game for Marquette," recalled radio play-by-play announcer Bob Bach, who was in his first season with the team. "Especially after losing to the Bearcats toward the end of the season." In their first tournament game, the Warriors were down by three points at the half, and as Marquette was heading back to its locker room, McGuire and forward Bernard Toone exchanged words about his playing time.

"The exchange was verbal," said Toone, who was usually the first man off the bench for Marquette. "We got chest to chest. There was a little shoving, and it really inspired me," explained Toone, who was restrained by Bo Ellis, while Hank Raymonds held onto McGuire. The only casualty was trainer Bob Weingart, who hurt his hand with all of the pushing and shoving in the locker room.

"Bernard and I had a verbal and physical get-together at the half," admitted McGuire. "But what that did was clear the decks and the rest of the tournament was a cakewalk."

"It was the standard Bernard-I'm-on-another-planet game," explained Bach, who noted that Toone had played a half-hearted first half. "Al had a guy who was not concentrating on the game. Bernard had fabulous skills. But the one thing that upset Al was players who had great talent and did not make full use of it."

The Warriors went on a 13-0 run in the second half, behind 18 points off the bench from a suddenly inspired Toone. "Butch Lee pointed at two Cincinnati players toward the end of the game," recalled Bach. "The Cincy players had mouthed off to Butch when Cincy beat Marquette near the end of the year, and Butch got even. And so did Marquette." The Warriors handled the Bearcats 66-51.

St. Patrick's Day found the Warriors in Oklahoma City for the Midwest Regional Semifinal against the Kansas State Wildcats. Up to this point, McGuire had not received a technical foul in the NCAA Tournament, but this game would prove different.

As the Warriors were running up the court, McGuire put his hand on his throat to let his players know that the Kansas State players were choking. But referee Jim Buckiewicz saw McGuire's signal and thought the coach was commenting on the officiating crew, and McGuire was hit with a technical. After that, McGuire was worrying about not only the game, but his future.

"After drawing the 'T' Al says to me, 'If we lose this game, I'm finished forever, Hank,'" recalled assistant coach Hank Raymonds.

The Warriors were down by 10 with just under 12 minutes left in the game when Raymonds made a suggestion to McGuire. "I told Al to put Jim Dudley in the game. He scored six points for us and got some key rebounds that turned the game around."

Dudley was joined by Toone as the sophomores started a 17-4 run for Marquette. Dudley then stole a pass and fed Butch Lee for a lay-up to give the Warriors a three-point lead with just 18 seconds remaining. The game was not over, however, as Bo Ellis fouled Kansas State's Darryl Winston as he was tipping in a rebound. The referees ruled the basket no good and awarded Winston two free throws. Winston made both free throws, but the Warriors still prevailed by a point, 67-66.

In the press conference after the game, McGuire delivered what was possibly the most emotional address of his coaching career, when he talked about the controversial technical foul, the NCAA's prepping of officials for the tournament, and his career. "After the game, Al went into the post-game interview room fuming," recalled Bach. "He was clearly on edge. He gave short, tight answers to reporters' questions, and then went on a 15-minute tirade. It was an impassioned plea to stop messing with McGuire and let his players play."

"I have a tremendous hang-up on the technical," McGuire began. "Either I'm sick-o or someone else is sick-o. Now, I was yelling that the Kansas State team was startin' to tighten up. I put my hand on my neck and says, 'They are tightening up.' And the ref blows a technical on me.

"I've been through this bullshit before, too many times in the NCAA . . . I coach exactly the same no matter where the hell I am, and every time I come to the NCAA, they end up calling technicals on me. Now it's absolutely wrong and I'm not a crybaby!

"I've been quiet for the last ten years. Now, either they're taking these officials and brainwashing them before they have my game. This has nothing to do with Kansas State. Kansas State should have beaten us. We were fortunate to win; we were lucky. Kansas State outplayed us, they were better prepared than we were, and they should have won the game. It just so happens we had a lot of time left and we caught them and we ended up getting a point or two ahead.

"The thing that got me aggravated is, I've been quiet about it for years. I've been through this thing from Athens, Georgia, with Ohio State, with Indiana, with them all! What the hell's going on? Guy calls a technical foul on me when I'm talking to the team, and the only way the guy can do it is because subconsciously he's been told, and then he won't come over and tell me. All I wanted to tell the guy is, 'Hey, I'm talking to the guys, not you.'

"Look, I'm 25 years in the business, guys. I've never said a word against officials. In 25 years, and I've gotta go through that crap again. That's 25 years, and I'm not lying. Take any player that follows me here. I've never said anything about officials. Under no conditions, anywhere, anytime.

"Now, there's too much smoke in back rooms, or too much whispering or too much something going on. We're not that good of a ball club, I admit that. But to call a technical foul at that time of a game is a mortal sin. It's WRONG!

"Now, I'm not a psycho. One technical foul all year on me. Don't you think Notre Dame, Michigan, Creighton, and Florida, and all these games are big games? We got three times as many people at the gosh-darn games. I don't do any different in this league than I do at home or on the road.

"We have big rivalries with the University of Wisconsin and Minnesota and Northwestern. What happens when I come to the NCAA? What are they trying to prove? Now, it doesn't make any difference to me. I'm on my way, but I don't want to blow it for these guys. I would not say a word if we lost. There was no way I could say a word. But I'm, I'm just to a point. Why do you think I made a statement last year? Why? I'm not an irrational person. I'm not an irresponsible person. But someone has to talk to somebody. I'm not looking for no breaks tomorrow night or any night. I never wanted a break from any official. I can't even tell you these guys' names.

"I have never rated an official in my life. I have never blackballed an official in my life. And I have never had a preference list in my life. In 13 years, I've never spoken to the commissioner's office. In 13 years! And I gotta come up here with the NCAA pulling this crap. And that's what it is. But that's a competent official. He wouldn't be here if he wasn't competent. And someone brainwashed him and they've been brainwashed before.

"And that's the reason I wouldn't coach anymore in the NCAA. It's . . . it's . . . it's been a zoo. Now I'll go by any rules and I should have gotten it off my chest seven years ago and left seven, nine years ago. It has nothing to do with the officials. I'm talking about when the subconscious of the official is reached. In some smoke-filled room. Somewhere they're prepping them. No official calls a technical foul on a guy. The official had his back to me running down the court. I'm yelling to the guys on my team. I'm saying, 'Hey, they're choking.' He turns around and blows a technical. And then he won't talk to me.

"So, peace. I got it off my chest and maybe it was me. It was a cancer and a pus that was in there the last ten years. So I'm glad it's out. And that's it. I'll never again say anything.

"I'm not talking about an individual official. I'm talking about the selection and the prepping of the officials before the game. That's what I'm talking about and they can have equal time and everything else they want.

"What the hell! A man spends 25 years of his life in a profession and every time he comes to something like this he looks like an idiot? Who the hell wants to look like an idiot out there? So, peace. I'm sorry and so on, but I'm glad to get it all off my chest.

"So, maybe I hurt some people. I'm sorry. But it's about time that some people started to realize that I'm not a bum in a bowery, or a wino in a hallway, or a pimp in a corner. I know my profession! And I know it well. And I've worked at it hard. All my life I worked at it hard. They won the game. They saved me from not being able to say this. Butch shouldn't have taken the last shot. I gave him hell for taking the last shot.

"I do not accept anything in victory that I won't accept in defeat. He had no right taking that last shot. The clock was more important. And that was it. Now they know what it is to play for me."

Paul Galvan, one of the Final Four officials that year, acknowledged that NCAA representatives do meet with officials before the games.

"In just about all NCAA tournaments, NCAA representatives on the tournament committee would always meet with the officials the day before the games for an hour or an hour and a half. At that time you would get the game assignment. And there is a Rule 10.9 on bench decorum, and we were told that it was to be strictly enforced," said Galvan, who worked Final Fours in 1975, '76, '77, '86, and '87. But '77 was the only year he worked the championship game. "The briefing officials never discussed before games that I've officiated that this coach does this or this team does that."

From then on, McGuire's memorable tirade became known as the "St. Patrick's Day speech," and could very well have been the spark the team needed in its next game against the Wake Forest Demon Deacons, on Saturday, March 19, at the Myriad Convention Center in Oklahoma City. "It was the most unforgettable thing I heard him say," recalled Bach.

While the Demon Deacons had a three-point cushion in the second half, Toone scored 9 of his 18 points during a 14-2 run that helped push the Warriors over the top. After a topsy-turvy relationship with McGuire that season, Toone led the team to a convincing 82-68 win. It meant the second Final Four for the Warriors in three years. The team was headed to Atlanta's Omni Arena, a.k.a. The Mecca of the South, to play in the Final Four.

As in previous tournament years, McGuire did not keep his players in the NCAA-sanctioned hotel. He housed his players in an as-yet-unopened Hilton Hotel away from the hubbub of Atlanta to keep distractions to a minimum. There was not even a pay phone on the premises.

"He bunched everyone else at the Radisson Hotel in Atlanta," remembered Norman Ochs. "Al made that the headquarters. But he found a hotel halfway around the circle. That way nobody could reach him or his team."

"On the day of the semifinals, I had eight people and Al said, 'I'll give you the tickets when I get to Atlanta.' At the Radisson, there was a young man from Milwaukee who holed himself up in a broom closet of the hotel, but did not have a ticket for the Final Four. Every time he saw McGuire, he reminded him about getting him a ticket."

The sunny Saturday semifinals featured UNLV and the University of North Carolina in the first game, followed by Marquette and the University of North Carolina–Charlotte, which had been a Division One basketball program only since 1972. Even though it was UNC–Charlotte's first NCAA Tournament, the 49ers had defeated a heavily-favored Michigan team to get to Atlanta.

"The atmosphere was exciting," recalled Bach. "I remember it wasn't what I had expected. I had the dual role of doing color and reporting on the games for WISN. I filed reports, et cetera. It was exhausting at the finals. I never did see UNLV play Carolina."

"The first game is starting at 12:30 p.m. and Al is still not dressed," Ochs recalled. "And Pat is looking for some privacy so she can get dressed."

"Al tells me, 'My secretary is bringing up 24 tickets.' The secretary walks in with the tickets. Al then says, 'I got one left over. Normy, give this to the guy in the broom closet. He hitchhiked all the way from Milwaukee.' The kid got a ticket. Al didn't even know the guy's name. Al thinks differently. He liked the kid's gumption, traveling all the way from Milwaukee and didn't have a ticket for the game.

"Before the game," Ochs continued, "McGuire tells Lee Rose, the coach of UNC–Charlotte, 'We've played a hundred schools with names like yours, but I'm not sure that we can beat your team.'"

Marquette was favored in the semifinal and started out accordingly. Unlike earlier contests, the Warriors sprinted out to a 23-9 lead against the 49ers. Marquette, however, lost a good deal of its lead when it went into its delay game.

"They were tight," McGuire said of UNCC after the game. "This was showtime. This was something they had never experienced before. All of a sudden they found themselves and played their game."

UNC–Charlotte went up 35-30 when Bo Ellis was whistled for his fourth foul with just over 14 minutes left in the game. The nip-and-tuck game started to go the Warriors' way when Jerome Whitehead scored six points in a 14-4 run to put Marquette back on top. Charlotte's team leader, guard Melvin Watkins, then fouled out with a minute left. Butch Lee hit a couple of jumpers, but Cedric "Cornbread" Maxwell tied the score at 49 with three seconds left in regulation.

McGuire called time and took a walk to the far end of the court, looking at the height of the Omni scoreboard.

"Al knew how high off the court the scoreboard was," recalled sports reporter Bill Jauss, who was covering the game for the *Chicago Tribune.* "He was just doing that to freeze UNC–Charlotte."

McGuire's excuse for the time-out was that he wanted to make sure that Butch Lee could launch a court-length pass without hitting the scoreboard, which was suspended above half court.

"McGuire was calm. He was exceedingly calm," recalled Greg Stack. "He came back and strolled to the bench. He said, 'Butch, you should have no problem throwin' it.' The pass was intended for Bo, but it went off his hands."

"I was the referee for the inbounds of the ball," said Galvan. "Charlie [Fouty of the Big Ten] was about at the free-throw line extended at the other end of the floor. I broke down court as Butch threw the ball. Then all of a sudden, the ball went up."

Lee flung a baseball pass down the court toward Bo Ellis's outstretched hands. The ball deflected off Ellis's hands to Jerome Whitehead who was being guarded by Maxwell. Whitehead turned and went up to dunk the ball, but the shot was partially blocked by Maxwell. The ball hit the backboard, bounced off the rim, and dropped through the net as time expired.

"Marquette University came to a complete silence with those three seconds," recalled Dan Kelly, a sophomore at the time, who was crammed into his dorm room with ten other students watching the game on a 12-inch color set.

Back in Atlanta, "It was very noisy," Galvan continued. "The minute the ball went in the basket there was total chaos. Players were jumping up and down. I was at the other end of the floor. When I turned, Al was coming toward me. I just stopped. Coach Rose was still in his bench area. I asked Chuck [referee Fouty] if he had heard the horn. Chuck said, 'No, I didn't hear the horn.' I counted the number of seconds, I thought I heard a horn, but I wasn't going to guess. If you're not sure, you're not gonna guess," explained Galvan, who was the trailing official on the play.

"McGuire was running out onto the court, he had his hands out to his sides saying, 'It's good! It's good! You've got to count the basket!' It wasn't in a threatening way," Galvan recalled of McGuire's pleadings.

"After the play, Al was there, two inches away from his [Galvan's] ear. 'Goaltending and a foul!' Al must have said it 50 times," Stack continued.

"Galvan told McGuire, 'If you move out of the way, I'll let you know if they're gonna count the basket.' In order to get down to where he could talk to me, he was bending down with his hands to the side.

"At that time you could feel the coliseum come to a hush. When there was not a signal, everyone started standing around and going toward the scorer's table. Everyone was wondering what I was going to do. I've always met with the timer and scorer. I told the timer, Larry Carter, at halftime and before the game, if I come to you, you have to tell me if the ball was in his hands or in the air."

When it was clear that Galvan was heading over to Carter at the scorer's table, McGuire made a beeline and cut off Coach Rose's access to the timer. "Al made his presence very clear at the scorer's table," remembered Pat Lloyd, a longtime Marquette season ticket-holder who sat with his wife, Polly, in front of the McGuire family at the Omni. "Al pushed him [Lee Rose] out of the way. Al was very demonstrative. We were in an SEC [Southeastern Conference] area. There were a lot of UNCC and UNC people there," noted Lloyd.

"You know that basket was good! You know that basket was good!" McGuire repeated as he interspersed what he called "tugboat" language in his sentences to emphasize his point. McGuire recalled that while he burned the timer's ears with his colorful words and phrases, Rose spoke in the manner of administrators who spend their time in ivory towers with the memos and pipes.

Galvan worked to get both coaches away from Carter, as McGuire persisted in his pleadings to count the basket. "Will you let me find out," said a frustrated Galvan, as he pushed both coaches about eight feet away from the scorer's table.

"It was a three-ring circus," remembered Bach. "I admired Galvan for the way in which he controlled the situation."

"I asked him twice," Galvan said of his queries to Carter, the timer. "'When the horn sounded, where was the ball? You're telling me when the horn sounded, the ball was in the basket.' I was at the head of the circle extension near the bench area. McGuire and Bernard Toone were standing behind me, with his hand above his head signaling, 'The basket's good! The basket's good!' [When Carter told me it was good] that was when I turned and made the signal that the basket was good and the game was over, Marquette had won."

Back in Milwaukee, "When the referee turned and dropped his arm," said Kelly, "Schroeder Hall began to shake. Kids went into ecstasy. Within minutes the dorm emptied."

"Lee Rose then asked me, 'Are you sure the basket counts?' 'Yes, it counts, Coach.' 'That was a good ball game. You called a good game,' he told me." Added Bob Bach, "Lee Rose was a wonderful gentleman. He got the word and left the court without a complaint."

The Marquette section of the Omni exploded in cheers as the 49ers' team and staff made their way to the locker room after congratulating McGuire and the Warriors. In a rare show of emotion, McGuire hugged Butch Lee after the basket was signaled good.

"David Cawood of the NCAA came in after the MU-UNCC game to get a statement from me to give to the press," remembered Galvan. "Al had not drawn any technical at that game. He and Coach Rose were excellent. Coach Rose took it as a gentleman. He took defeat as an outstanding coach and professional."

"After Marquette had beaten UNC–Charlotte," said Bach, "I remember leaving the arena that day overhearing the University of North Carolina fans saying they were not going to have any problems with Marquette." "We took a lot of taunting from the ACC fans those two days," added Pat Lloyd. "They told us, 'Wait till you play the real North Carolina on Monday night. Wait till you see the real Tar Heels. It's gonna be a different story.' We said, 'Wait till you see this independent team from the Midwest.'"

Back in Milwaukee, students continued to spill out of the dorms and bars and onto Wisconsin Avenue down to Lake Michigan to celebrate as they had for previous NCAA and NIT victories. Ten thousand students poured down Wisconsin Avenue. While the championship game was not until Monday night, the opportunity to celebrate a big win was too good to pass up. "People were stopped in the middle of Wisconsin Avenue screaming for several hours," remembered Kelly, who added that even though the bars were filled, there was a "nervous, excited anticipation of the grand finale on Monday night."

That night the sports programs in Milwaukee and throughout the country were talking about those improbable three seconds. The UNC-UNLV game, which UNC won 84-83, was given second billing in most sportscasts. "That was probably the most replayed three seconds in the history of college basketball," McGuire said after the game.

Both Marquette and North Carolina had Sunday to practice for Monday night's final. McGuire and Hank Raymonds put in a game plan they thought might work. They decided to put in their own delay game. After seeing how quickly the team picked up the new wrinkle, Raymonds and McGuire said of Carolina's famed Four Corners Offense, "Bring it on."

"Around the game itself," recalled Bach, "I seemed to remember the Marquette players appearing as if they were great underdogs. There was an 'us versus them' mentality. Marquette's shootarounds were loosely structured. They were businesslike, but very relaxed. They didn't seem to be in awe of the place."

On Championship Monday, McGuire decided to get away from it all and take off on his motorcycle. He wound up heading to Social Circle, Georgia, outside of Atlanta, where former NFL quarterback great and Medalist "coach" Norm "The Dutchman" Van Brocklin had a pecan farm.

"When I arrived," recalled McGuire, "the Dutchman thought that I was the veterinarian there to deliver his calves. I said to him, 'Hey, who the hell do you think I am? This is Al.' The Dutchman was rough. He thought his players were spending too much time with the hookers downtown."

"He [Van Brocklin] showed Al around the farm, showed him how the farm operated," noted Norman Ochs. "After a while, McGuire looked at his watch and said, 'I'd better get started back downtown.'"

As the story goes, McGuire was late getting back to Atlanta and was stuck in traffic. "There was a traffic jam near the Omni," continued Ochs, who was on his way to the game at the time. "And I look over to the left of me in traffic, and there's Al, sitting in a friend's car heading to the game!"

Earlier that day, James Sankovitz, Marquette vice president of government relations, had been sent to the airport to pick up Wisconsin Gov. Patrick Lucey for the game. When switching planes in Detroit, Gov. Lucey had met University of Wisconsin coach "Badger Bob" Johnson, who was preparing his team for the NCAA hockey finals. When asked why he was going to the NCAA basketball championship, Gov. Lucey simply told Johnson, "Because they invited me."

"We take the trooper car into the Omni," continued Sankovitz, "and there's Al, walking by himself toward the arena. He says, 'Hello, Governor.' The governor then says, 'Why aren't you with your team?' 'They know what they have to do. I'm not sure I know what I have to do,' replied Al, and he kept walking."

At first, the Omni security people refused to let McGuire in because he had no identification to prove he was indeed Al McGuire. Besides, there were reports that a Dean Smith impersonator had crashed a number of NCAA parties throughout the weekend, and the security detail at the Omni was not taking any chances, especially with some guy claiming to be Al McGuire.

Finally, Hank Raymonds arrived to vouch for Al, and the coach was allowed in for his last game as coach. "He was always late, anyway," shrugged Raymonds.

NBC was preparing for the 8 p.m. tip-off with Dick Enberg, Curt Gowdy, and Billy Packer ready to call the action. Enberg described the game as McGuire's "Auld Lang Syne," and Gowdy said of McGuire, "He's the most quoted, most colorful, and most controversial coach in the game, but he's been a winner all the way."

Each coach was then given an opportunity to say a few words before the game. Dressed in three-piece suits, they looked like salesmen instead of basketball coaches. Smith wore sideburns just like some of the players, although Bo Ellis wore the mutton-chop style favored by many ballplayers in the late 1970s.

Carolina's Smith complimented Marquette, calling the team "the best rebounding team in the country," and noted that Ellis was the "smartest and quickest defensive player in the country."

McGuire said, "The [Marquette players] paid the maximum price to get here. I feel they are on top of their game. I think it will be a dynamite game. No way will I blow it with a technical. Milwaukee, we're heading back home tonight, and I hope with a big trophy."

Smith's Tar Heels, though a slight favorite in the championship game, had to play without center Tom LaGarde. "[Walter] Davis had played with a broken finger. [Phil] Ford couldn't shoot from outside with his bad elbow," said Smith, who was coaching his fifth career Final Four. "I had no idea how we'd come out over UNLV."

While there certainly was a great deal of sentiment for McGuire, since he was coaching in his final game, quite a few people in the basketball fraternity were pulling for Smith to finally win the brass ring after so many trips to the Final Four.

In Milwaukee, half-barrels of beer flowed in every TV lounge on the Marquette campus. There was a sprinkling of rain in the early evening, and at game time there was a nervous excitement, according to Kelly.

Officiating the game were Reggie Copeland and Galvan, who had refereed the 1974 Final Four contest between UCLA and North Carolina State, eventual winner over Marquette in the Finals. "That [UCLA-NC State] game was very memorable because North Carolina State upset UCLA," said Galvan. "Players like Walton, [David] Thompson, who were NCAA greats. It was a great basketball game with great talent.

"But 1977 perhaps was the memorable one. That was the only one where I refereed the championship game. And since these were the last games of a great basketball coach, that made them memorable. That was a big news item with him, with the press. This was his [McGuire's] last tournament. After the semifinal game, I'm assuming that everyone was rooting for him to go out as a champion. Playing North Carolina, with another great coach, Dean Smith, it was memorable.

"To an official, working in the NCAA championship is like the Super Bowl. To be selected is an honor, regardless of whether it's a semifinal or a championship," noted Galvan, who said to McGuire before the game that he hoped that the championship would not end like Saturday afternoon's game. "He seemed more relaxed in the championship game than in the semifinal game. He was relieved he was in the championship game."

A soft rain began falling in Atlanta just before the game started. Marquette won the tip-off, and both teams started out tight with Bo Ellis missing a jump hook and the Tar Heels being whistled for a three-second violation.

The game's first points were scored on a free throw by Carolina's Mike O'Koren. Ellis scored the game's first field goal, but picked up two quick fouls, forcing McGuire to switch to a 2-3 zone to protect Ellis, the only Marquette player ever to play in two Final Fours.

The confident Butch Lee was smooth on the floor with his stutter-step dribble drives and was "always in control," according to Enberg. "Butch Lee had a level of self-confidence unmatched by any other guard," marveled Bach.

Marquette's trapping defense forced Davis into two quick fouls. Not long after, Phil Ford scored the Tar Heels' first field goal. During the first television time-out, the horn-heavy strains of Chase's "Get It On" could be heard as the network went to break. McGuire had his arms up, directing from the sidelines. Smith and a limping McGuire met with Galvan to question a foul call. McGuire had hurt his foot kicking the scorer's table after a call he thought was questionable.

"We had a foul, then a false common foul and a dead ball foul," explained Galvan. "They don't shoot those technicals. I had to explain why they were not going to shoot the free throws. They [coaches] mostly listened. I got both together to explain it."

It seemed that on this night, Butch Lee's jumpers were falling easily. Early in the game, Carolina seemed to be getting a few second-chance points. But after Warrior sharpshooter Gary Rosenberger checked in, the Warriors switched to a 2-1-2 zone. Up to that point, it was a nip-and-tuck contest.

Rosenberger hit his first shot, a long-range jumper, to give the Warriors a 12-11 lead after ten minutes of the first half. Marquette stayed in the zone and began playing big under the boards.

With just over six minutes to go in the half, Marquette went into a stall, which best utilized Lee's one-on-one moves and helped put the Warriors up 21-20 with 6:30 left. Marquette stayed in a zone, this time switching back to the 2-1-2.

At the 5:28 mark, Davis picked up his third foul and Bo Ellis was starting to make his presence known with rebounding and shooting. Enberg described him as "lightning in a bottle."

Behind Ellis, Marquette increased its lead to 11 points as the chants of "WE ARE MARQUETTE" echoed throughout the Omni. At about that time, drops of rain began to fall from the ceiling and formed slick spots on the court. With 1:38 left, Marquette continued to play keep-away, but a Warrior was called for a foul. "What foul?" McGuire asked as he got off the bench.

Carolina's John Kuester looked exhausted as he headed to the free-throw line. After the free throws, Butch Lee went coast-to-coast to give Marquette a 12-point cushion. McGuire almost fell out of his chair, and the Warriors went into the locker room leading 39-27.

" 'Okay, fellas, you're halfway home," McGuire began his final half-time talk. "Do not get overconfident. These guys are gonna come back,' " team manager Greg Stack recalled the coach telling the team. "Al was afraid because of the lead, there was gonna be a letdown. He predicted that if that happened, Dean would go to the Four Corners offense. We spent a helluva lot of time on the Four Corners."

McGuire said later that the Warriors probably played the best 20 minutes of basketball in his 25 years of coaching—especially defensively, where he thought his team was on top of it. He was also surprised by the 39 points his team scored in the first half.

Warrior fans on the Marquette campus were cautiously optimistic as the second half began, even though the half-barrels on hand were quickly running out, as well as at the local liquor stores. And the rain began to fall a little harder in Milwaukee.

Watching the game in his mom's living room in Mt. Pleasant, Michigan, was an impressionable 11-year-old named Tom Crean. Marquette was the team he had adopted during the NCAA Tournament. Marquette and Al McGuire became synonymous for him during the Warriors' magical journey to the national championship. In fact, Crean has stated that it was Marquette's national championship that was among his first memories of watching college basketball. From that point forward, he was hooked on Marquette.

North Carolina won the tip to start the second half and the Warriors opened in a man-to-man defense. O'Koren scored the first field goal and blocked a Butch Lee shot on the other end. When O'Koren appeared to double-dribble in front of the Marquette bench, McGuire complained strongly to Galvan.

The Tar Heels whittled Marquette's lead to 39-31 on another O'Koren jumper off a Warrior turnover. McGuire quickly called time to stem the Tar Heel tide.

After another basket gave North Carolina a 6-0 run to start the half, the Tar Heels went to a full-court press. The teams traded baskets, and then a foul was called on Marquette, which sprang McGuire from his seat and set him to pacing, strutting, hands on hips, looking up and down the scorer's table. Another O'Koren jumper trimmed the margin to 41-37.

McGuire pointed and yelled, asking for a time-out. He was yelling at the officials, "What's going on?" His square face was taut with anger. Frustration was setting in for McGuire as his Warriors went cold during a 10-1 Carolina run.

After the time-out, Marquette came out in a zone, but Tar Heel zone-breaker John Kuester hit again to narrow the margin 41-39. The Warriors' troubles continued. Walter Davis tied the game at 41. McGuire orchestrated the offense from the bench as North Carolina then went into a zone. The Warriors turned the ball over and the Tar Heels extended their second-half run to 14-2.

Jim Boylan broke the Marquette dry spell with a jumper to put the Warriors ahead 43-41. McGuire kept his team in a 1-2-2 zone, but Davis tied the game again at 43. Smith countered with a 1-3-1 zone and Carolina scored off a Tom Zaliagiris steal to take the lead for the first time since early in the first half, 45-43.

NBC analyst Billy Packer predicted that Smith would soon go to his Four Corners offense. Marquette initially returned to a man-to-man defense with just under 13 minutes left and tied the game at 45. McGuire switched to a 1-2-2 zone and Smith, as expected, went into his Four Corners.

McGuire then began orchestrating from the sidelines, gesturing to his players to back up and then come back to defend Carolina. Since the game was tied, the defensive team, Marquette, still had to come after the offense at the five-second count. McGuire said that he was "Mickey Mousing" Smith's Four Corners.

"I think, several times, I know North Carolina had the ball, and McGuire would always say to me, 'We don't have to go out, do we?' I'd nod my head. He kept his bunch back and stayed within the rule," remembered referee Galvan.

"I wanted to pull them [Marquette] out of the zone," recalled Smith.

"We'd gone to the Four Corners every game we were ahead. Al was smart, and he didn't come out. We thought we'd get one [basket]."

McGuire remained in what he called a one-man zone defense with his "aircraft carrier," 6'10" center Jerome "J" Whitehead, underneath the basket, to cut off any backdoor opportunities for Carolina. McGuire coolly continued to direct his players from the sidelines.

"He's like Leonard Bernstein, a little more from the woodwinds," said Dick Enberg, commenting on McGuire's own brand of conducting during the two minutes that Smith had stayed with his delay game. Over that period of time, North Carolina had still not taken a shot. "It dried their sweat and they lost their momentum," said McGuire.

Marquette was able to get the ball back, and Jim Boylan gave the Warriors a 47-45 lead with 8:22 left. Bernard Toone pulled down a rebound on a Walter Davis miss. The teams exchanged turnovers as Phil Ford gave it to Butch Lee, and then Lee gave it right back.

Ford attempted to save a ball from going out of bounds. When he did not immediately get back to the court, McGuire asked the officials to wait until Ford was ready to rejoin his teammates. "Classy gesture," complimented Packer.

There were seven minutes left and Marquette turned the ball over on a bad Lee pass into the paint. Boylan then fouled Davis, who tied the game at 47. Marquette took the lead at 49-47 and then went up 51-47 when Davis goal-tended on a Boylan lay-up.

Marquette went to a 1-2-2 zone as Carolina inbounded with 5:20 left in the game. Lee missed a lay-up and Kuester hit a jumper to narrow Marquette's lead to 51-49. Carolina then went to a full-court press. Bo Ellis drove the lane beautifully and was fouled by Kuester.

At the 3:43 mark, Boylan slipped on the Omni court made slick by the water dripping from the arena ceiling. Carolina got the ball on the Marquette turnover, but Whitehead stole it back for the Warriors and McGuire called a time-out with 2:28 left.

All of the Marquette players stood around McGuire, who addressed each of them. All eyes were on the coach as he gestured, put his hands on the shoulders and heads of the players as he made his point. Just as the huddle broke, he pulled Whitehead aside.

With Marquette leading 51-49, Kuester fouled Lee and fouled out of the game. With exactly two minutes remaining, McGuire put in his own Four Corners offense, and Whitehead was fouled in the bonus situation. Then came a television time-out.

Whitehead made both free throws to give Marquette a 53-49 lead with 1:56 left. Everything seemed to be going Marquette's way, until Bernard Toone was fouled, poked in the eye by O'Koren. When Toone swung his elbows in retaliation, Lee tried to restrain him from an altercation, but a technical foul was called against Toone. McGuire put his hands to his head in disbelief. "I do remember having to tell Toone to just play," said Galvan. "'Let's play ball and let's cut that stuff out,' I told him. He [Toone] didn't have a negative attitude the rest of the night."

Toone missed his free throws. Davis made the technicals for Carolina. Smith then argued his case with the referee as Marquette team captain Bo Ellis looked on. Marquette still led 53-51.

McGuire asked Galvan to explain the double foul and jump ball. Al bent over, then started clapping after speaking with the referee. Marquette won the subsequent jump ball and O'Koren fouled Boylan, who hit both free throws for a 55-51 Marquette lead, with 1:25 left.

Ellis was then fouled by Davis while going for a rebound. Ellis hit both free throws for a 57-51 lead. Davis then went coast to coast for a lay-up, narrowing the lead to 57-53.

Marquette's band began to play the school fight song, "Ring Out Ahoya!" O'Koren fouled out and Ellis hit both free throws for a 59-53 lead with 1:02 left. Davis was fouled by Ellis and hit one of two free throws. Marquette led 59-54 with 47 seconds left.

McGuire looked up at the clock. He seemed to be taking in every remaining second of the game, remembering what was happening as the seconds ticked away from his coaching career. Phil Ford fouled Rosenberger, who made both shots for a 61-55 margin. Butch Lee then drove in for a lay-up, which clinched the game. Marquette had a 63-55 lead with 26 second left. As he walked along the sidelines, McGuire pumped his fist in a quick, downward motion, as if to say, "That's all she wrote." He knew then that he had the championship.

McGuire put up one finger, pointing out what needed to be done. Signaling to his players with his hands, he was still coaching, even with the game in the bag.

With 19 seconds left, McGuire was still looking at the clock. Marquette fans broke out their gold pom-pons. Jim Boylan hit two free throws, giving Marquette a 10-point lead. McGuire continued to look at the clock. He pointed at the clock as Rosenberger looked at it with him. The Warrior lead was 65-57.

With 11 seconds left, North Carolina fouled again. At eight seconds, McGuire's eyes began to tear up. "It's tough for him to show his emotions," noted Dick Enberg, as the crowd began to chant, "We Want Al. We Want Al. We Want Al. We Want Al."

In Milwaukee, "I turned off the volume on our set," said Kelly. "At that moment, you could feel Schroeder Hall shaking."

"We may have had a time-out and I looked down and he had his hands in his face," recalled Galvan. "I remember saying to myself, that's a great accomplishment, to win a national championship. He was into every tick of the clock. I'm glad I was a part of this," said Galvan, who added that he did not let McGuire's last game distract him from the task at hand.

McGuire buried his head in a towel as Hank Raymonds put his arm around his shoulders and gave him a congratulatory hug. Then McGuire wiped his eyes and Raymonds and Majerus shook hands with each other on the bench. Raymonds tightened his rolled-up program and punched the air with it.

Marquette's lead was 67-57, as Lee deflected a pass out of bounds. Davis then scored the last basket of the game, giving Marquette its final margin of victory, 67-59, and its first national championship. Marquette was the last independent to win a national basketball championship. Dean Smith rushed over to shake McGuire's hand, as Bo Ellis began cutting down one of the nets. He thrust his arm through the hoop in celebration. "Basketball's Don Quixote," declared Enberg, as McGuire began to accept the congratulations of his family and friends.

In Milwaukee, "Ten thousand kids overflowed with jubilation down Wisconsin Avenue," recalled Kelly, who joined the run down to Lake Michigan in the steady rain that night. "I sat on the trunk of a Buick Regal with five other guys and a girl. Eight kids on the hood and the driver had to lean his head out the window in order to drive."

Back in New York, McGuire's brother Dick was watching at home and kept repeating, "I can't believe it's happening to Alfred McGuire."

"As Al passed me on the way to the locker room," recalled former Marquette SID Jim Foley, "he said, 'Jim, you changed your hair.'" While McGuire was taking in his greatest moment, he somehow was able to deflect attention from himself.

From there he went into the locker room, where the only person with him was Marquette SID Kevin Byrne. When asked why he was going there during the celebration, he replied, "I'm not ashamed to cry. I just want to cry alone."

When he returned to the court, coach of the national champions, he smiled broadly and exchanged hugs with family and players. It was his moment, but he wanted to share it with the players.

In the post-game press conference, McGuire's simple explanation for the win was that North Carolina "fell apart in the second half. We hung in there."

When asked how he felt, McGuire replied, "Emotionally drained. I'm pleased for the guys. It doesn't seem real. Ya know, you think about something like this, but I've always been an alley fighter. I don't usually get into the silk lace situations. It seems like it is preordained, but I don't like to use the words of the TV announcers, the clichés.

"I was not emotional until a five-second count triggered me. I trigger easily. As a coach, you have to be constantly alert. Right now, I feel washed out. Once the avalanche came and we were tied [at the start of the second half], I tried to stop the avalanche by delays and I called time-outs, or something like that. You have to stop the momentum, no matter what.

"At the end of the game, I sat there and thought of all the locker rooms, the dirty jocks, the PALs [Police Athletic Leagues], and the other things that a New York street fighter knows when growing up."

With Al McGuire, it was life imitating art, as later that evening Sylvester Stallone would pick up the Oscar for best picture at the Academy Awards in Hollywood for his film, *Rocky*. Al McGuire was one of those fighters of the world whom Stallone thanked for his inspiration in his acceptance speech. Also, the rock group Queen had just released a new single, "We Are the Champions," which was quickly edited into a video by Marquette's WMUR-TV staff. It eventually aired on all of Milwaukee's local television stations.

"I was happy for Al," said Dean Smith. "I thought they played extremely well. Al was smart and he didn't come out [for the Four Corners]. We thought we'd get one [basket]. Ellis blocked Bruce Buckley. He's certainly a great coach. He has a good feel for the game. He just goes with the flow. His way was best for him. He definitely kept you from doing what you wanted to do during a game."

"There were more North Carolina fans that night at the championship," recalled Pat Lloyd. "But even after the game, the Carolina fans complimented us as we left. It rained pretty hard, but no one mentioned it. A lot of the fans came back with us on the charter flight. People were handing out 'Al McGuire for President' buttons."

"In the locker room, Al cut me a piece of the basketball net," recalled John Fedders, a longtime friend and attorney for McGuire. "Al touched people on the cheeks as he was thanking each of us. He was also hugging each of us. When we were on the bus heading to the airport, Al turned to me and said that he hadn't had anything to eat. 'John, can you get me a couple of hot dogs?' When we arrived at the airport, I went out and brought the hot dogs back for Al."

In Milwaukee, the rains continued to fall steadily all evening, as it seemed that every one of Marquette's 12,000-plus students stormed Wisconsin Avenue. Climbing on top of light poles, jumping on top of cars and taxis, riding on top of city buses, hanging from traffic signals and business shingles. "Students climbed on top of Milwaukee buses and walked the length of the bus roof from back to front," recalled Dan Kelly.

The 1600 block of Wells Street was a solid mass of reveling students. "Within hours, the campus bars were drunk dry," continued Kelly.

It was difficult to get a phone call into Milwaukee that night because it seemed that all the lines were busy and all the lights were on.

The students began running to Lake Michigan to celebrate the city's first national championship since the Milwaukee Bucks won the NBA title back in 1971, six years earlier. The city, however, had not seen a celebration this wild since the old Milwaukee Braves beat the New York Yankees to win the 1957 World Series. On the minus side, the celebration cost the city more than $11,000 in damages.

"The effect that the team had was to send Milwaukee into delirium," recalled Bob Bach. "It was evidenced best when the team returned to Milwaukee. At 2, 2:30 in the morning, fans had jammed the Mitchell Field [airport] concourse. It was wall-to-wall people. They had been drinking. It was scary. I was not pleased to be in the middle.

"Jay Whitehead had tears in his eyes. You had no control over where you were going. The team had their uniforms stolen. The positive was that it put Milwaukee on the map. The fact that he won it in his last game was the zenith," Bach said. McGuire had wisely ducked out a back gate to avoid the crush of the fans.

Neil Milbert of the *Chicago Tribune* was assigned to do a story on local reaction to the NCAA Final in Milwaukee. He was stationed in a hotel atop a hill at 18th Street and Wisconsin Avenue, where he watched the game in a hotel room.

"After the game I drove to Mitchell Field, where the team plane was to arrive," recalled Milbert. "I was talking to Al at the airport and we got swept up in the wave of people who crammed the concourse. Al, Allie, and a couple of priests and I were able to duck downstairs away from the crowds. We wound up in a little dank room in the basement of the airport drinking coffee out of small plastic cups at two in the morning. It was so crowded [that night] Wisconsin Gov. Patrick Lucey lost his chauffeur."

Students driving back from the airport followed *Milwaukee Sentinel* newspaper trucks as they dropped papers at each vending box throughout the city and took every paper from the boxes as souvenirs. At McCormick Hall that night, it appeared that torches were being tossed out of the dorm's windows. But the flames were coming from telephone books set ablaze. The flagpole at McCormick Hall was toppled. After the game, another student took his black-and-white television, opened the window, and let it drop. Asked to explain why, he said: "It was the most beautiful thing I had ever seen and I'll never see anything on that television as beautiful again."

Many students did not attend class the next day. Many did not get up until rather late the next day. And when they did, they discovered that

Marquette University President Rev. Raynor had not canceled classes. A pep rally was held on campus a few days later, where a tired Al McGuire and players were honored by the school for their accomplishment. McGuire, a happy Warrior, thanked everyone from his co-coaches to the university to the players and the fans.

Toward the end of the press conference, someone reminded McGuire about an engagement he had made before the tournament. "Al, I guess our lunch is off again for next Friday." McGuire said, "I'll be there. You buyin'?" "Yeah." "I'll be there."

McGuire received a congratulatory phone call from his mother, Winifred, saying how proud she was and, "Alfie, I'm glad ya got out clean."

After the game, McGuire told a friend, "I'll be talking for the next ten years." ∎

CHAPTER ONE:
THE TORCH IS PASSED: EMBRACING THE McGUIRE LEGACY

In the years following Marquette's One Shining Moment, the basketball program had experienced its share of hits and misses in post-season play.

After Al McGuire went on to stardom as a network basketball analyst, Marquette's basketball program saw five coaches come and go, trying to live up to the massive legacy he left behind in Milwaukee. None had succeeded in stepping out of his long shadow, and only two had averaged at least 20 wins during their respective tenures: Hank Raymonds (21, 1978–83) and Mike Deane (20, 1994–99).

Between the national championship and the 1998–99 season, Marquette University's basketball program was basically treading water. Marquette appeared in nine NCAA Tournaments and as many National Invitation Tournaments. Marquette won a total of five NCAA games in that span, advancing as far as the Sweet 16 just once (1994). Among its 10 NIT wins was a runner-up finish in 1995.

Marquette's loyal fan base had held steady at the old Milwaukee Arena and in the NBA-ready Bradley Center (which opened in 1988) in the days A.M. (After McGuire). But with infrequent tournament appearances and a lack of television coverage, Marquette had virtually disappeared from college basketball's Top 25 rankings and was flying under the national radar. The result: a paucity of "blue chip" recruits.

In the late 1980s, two key changes were made that ultimately paved the way for a new direction in the basketball program. The first was hiring the experienced Bill Cords as athletic director. The second was the decision to leave the dwindling ranks of the former Great Independents to join a conference. The thinking was that conference affiliation would increase national television exposure, opening up recruiting pipelines, and offer more opportunities for NCAA Tournament bids.

After two tries at conference affiliation (Midwestern Collegiate in 1989; Great Midwest in 1991), the third time proved to be the charm for Marquette with Conference USA. Prior to the 1995–96 season, Marquette joined Louisville, Cincinnati, Memphis, DePaul, St. Louis, as well as some refugees from other defunct conferences, including the Southwest and Metro.

The high point for Marquette basketball attendance was the 1993–94 season, when it averaged 14,347 per game at the Bradley Center. That Sweet 16 season was the last for coach Kevin O'Neill, who lit out for the University of Tennessee, and also the last season for the school nickname "Warriors." The decision to make the change came during the administration of President Albert J. DiUlio, S.J. From that point forward, Marquette's sports teams have been known as the Golden Eagles, which was a sore point of contention among many students, longtime alumni, and basketball fans in Milwaukee.

In the next five years under O'Neill's successor, Mike Deane, attendance trended up and down, topping out at 12,247 in his third season. It was during this period that Marquette even lost its own holiday tournament, also known as the Milwaukee Classic and First Bank Classic (now Blue & Gold Classic)—twice—which was anathema to the diehard fans in Milwaukee.

"Mike Deane liked to recruit coaches' sons (Mike Bargen, Bart Miller)," recalled Bob Berghaus, who covered Marquette for the *Milwaukee Journal Sentinel* back then. "He liked good students, and Brian Wardle was his biggest recruit." Noted Deane, "Every guy that I recruited completed his degree requirements in May of his last year."

As Marquette went through its starts and stops in post-season play, fans were beginning to wonder—as were the local and national media—

if Marquette's glory days would ever return. It seemed as if every other year the press was asking who was going to be the next Al McGuire. It was the obligatory question after each new Marquette coach was introduced.

While Marquette did make consecutive NCAA Tournament appearances in 1996 and 1997, it advanced only as far as the second round in '96. The Golden Eagles finished the 1995–96 season ranked No. 20 in the country, and the '97 squad won four games in four days to take the Conference USA Tournament Championship. Marquette was only the second team to accomplish such a feat up to that time. The first was Auburn, when it won the 1985 SEC Tournament Championship. "Deane was an excellent strategist," commented Berghaus, who added that the coach always found a way to stop the opposing team's best player.

Marquette advanced to the third round of the NIT during the 1997–98 season, before losing to Minnesota 73-71. It was about that time that Deane said, "Marquette was not a program that people should expect every year that they could contend for a national championship. But on occasion, if they got the right group of kids, they could do well. In today's competitive environment, you can't expect that you're going to have the same advantages that other major schools have. Private schools, like Marquette, are at a disadvantage. The goal every year is to make the NCAA Tournament. But some of the fans in major conferences turn their nose up at the NIT." Marquette fans, however, had higher expectations for the program, and were not about to settle for annual trips to the NIT.

There would be no post-season following that 1998–99 campaign. Marquette finished the season a disappointing 14-15, which dropped the team into the cellar of the American Division of C-USA. Even though Deane had won 100 games during his tenure and his teams defeated perennial conference powerhouse Cincinnati five times, Marquette could not make the leap to the next level of college basketball's elite. Bill Cords felt it was time for a change and dismissed Deane.

"I received e-mails and letters as it began to be clear we were changing coaches," noted Rev. Wild. " 'What is going on here? Are we going to hurt the program?' They [longtime fans] feared a downtown of the program."

The firing of Deane surprised many, including some of the veteran players who were not sure they would stay in Milwaukee when a new coach was named. Those players who were sitting on a fence decided to take a wait-and-see attitude before making the decision to leave Milwaukee, which would have resulted in a lost year of eligibility for each of them. Deane's only signed recruit for the 1999–2000 season, Krunti Hester of Indianapolis, stayed at Marquette that season and then transferred to Lamar University in Beaumont, Texas, where Deane was next hired.

That March, the Bradley Center played host to the first two rounds of the NCAA Midwest Regionals. One of the participating schools was Michigan State University, which was expected to make a deep run in the '99 Tournament. The Spartans first game was Friday night, March 12, against venerable Jim Phelan's Mount St. Mary's Mountaineers.

It was during Michigan State's scheduled practice time at the Bradley Center that Bill Cords happened to be paying close attention to the Spartans' pre-game ritual.

And he liked what he saw.

Cords watched the young associate head coach for MSU put the Spartans through their paces and was impressed with the energy, enthusiasm, discipline, and organization with which the coach conducted the workout.

Cords liked so much of what he saw that he requested permission from Michigan State athletic director Merritt Norvell Jr. to talk to the coach: 33-year-old Tom Crean. In fact, MSU and Tom Izzo allowed Marquette to talk to Crean during the Spartans' NCAA Tournament run.

"When Tom met with the group [selection committee] he blew their socks off," recalled Rev. Wild. "He really impressed them. I received a call from one of the committee members who said 'I think we have our man.'"

"While it was a risk, he seemed to bring a great deal to the table," continued Rev. Wild. "One of the concerns was would he be a good game coach, because Tom had never been a head coach before. Everyone knew he would be a good recruiter."

Cords and Rev. Robert A. Wild, S.J., Marquette president, went to East Lansing to meet with Crean and his wife, the former Joani Harbaugh. "I was impressed that Tom wanted to involve Joani in this decision," said Rev. Wild, who came away impressed with Crean as a person.

At the time, Crean was going through his own version of March Madness. First, he helped MSU head coach Tom Izzo lead the Spartans to their first Final Four in 20 years. Then Cords offered Crean the top job at Marquette. Cords did not have to wait long for his answer.

On March 30, 1999, Tom Crean signed a five-year contract to become the 15th coach in Marquette basketball history. Unbeknownst to Cords, the new coach already knew something about the school's basketball history. When Crean was a youngster growing up in Mt. Pleasant, MI, he wrote to Marquette every year after the '77 championship, requesting a copy of the team media guide. In his annual letters to the MU sports information director, the young Crean stated that he was Marquette's biggest fan. At least in the state of Michigan.

"Very early in this search, we focused in on Tom Crean," said Rev. Wild, "because we realized he possessed everything we were looking for— great recruiting ability, knowledge of the Midwest, successful coaching experience, a tremendous work ethic—and he shared our vision for what this program is capable of achieving." Rev. Wild, who was named Marquette president in 1996, was a professor at the university during the 1970s and experienced the basketball program's glory days firsthand during the McGuire Era.

There was surprise after the Crean hiring was announced. After all, his name was not among those being floated in the sports media. Tony Barone of Texas A&M, Quin Snyder, Steve Alford, and even Kevin O'Neill were some of the names being mentioned. However, among college basketball cognoscenti, Crean was a well-known entity, and many of the pundits and analysts were offering hosannas to both Crean and Marquette for making the match.

"No name lit up," said Marquette President Rev. Robert A. Wild. "Some of the bigger name coaches couldn't be pried from their jobs. We ended up narrowing the search to some senior assistant coaches, of whom Tom was one."

Crean was introduced to the media at the university's Alumni Memorial Union. When it was Crean's turn to speak, he said all of the right things, but his talk did not sound practiced. He sounded sincere. He exuded confidence, an infectious enthusiasm, and he made it clear that he would leave no stone unturned in his efforts to make the basketball program a source of pride for the university once again. Crean's integrity was palpable, and listening to him speak, one wanted to believe what Crean believed. It was obvious he was loyal, dedicated, and committed to the task at hand.

"I am very excited about coming to Marquette and beginning a new chapter here. I'm coming with great enthusiasm and a willingness to work as hard as it takes to help the university and the program keep achieving excellence. I can't tell you what it means to have a chance to walk into a program that is synonymous with the success it's had and the tradition it's had."

"After Coach Crean was introduced at the Union, we walked right up and introduced ourselves," recalled longtime season-ticket holder Larry Six of Mukwonago, Wisconsin. "Five days later, a call was on my business phone line from Coach Crean, and he said, 'Hi, Larry, I met you and your son at the Union last week and wanted to thank you for coming. If you have any suggestions for improving the basketball program, please let me know.' That's when I knew that he was different from any other coaches," said an impressed Six.

"There were people who were concerned that Marquette was going to downgrade the program," continued Rev. Wild. "What we wanted to do was strengthen and improve. That we could do a lot better. The goal is to get to the NCAA Tournament on a regular basis. That was a good way of thinking about the quality of the program. Normally, that would be a part of a quality program.

"We knew we needed to give Tom time, but keep fans' expectations out. We knew it would take probably three years before we saw results. Players were initially concerned about the coaching change. But after Tom met with the players, people were starting to sing a different tune. The players had to get used to a more structured practice, workout and academic routine," said Rev. Wild.

What is often forgotten about McGuire's hiring is that he was not mentioned as a favorite for the position 35 years earlier. When it was announced that a McGuire was taking over Marquette basketball, fans in Milwaukee thought it was Frank McGuire whom Marquette was hiring in 1964 to replace the fired Eddie Hickey.

Like McGuire, Crean had paid his coaching dues. As an undergraduate at Central Michigan University, he worked as a part-time coach at

Alma College and at Mt. Pleasant High School, his alma mater. Crean's annual salary for his work at Alma was $500 a year.

Before the 1989–90 season, it was then Michigan State head coach Jud Heathcote who gave Crean his start in Division I when he hired him as a graduate assistant. Other assistants on that staff included Izzo and Kelvin Sampson.

The next season, Crean was hired as an assistant on Ralph Willard's staff at Western Kentucky before following Willard to the University of Pittsburgh in 1994. After one year at Pitt, Crean returned to Michigan State where he worked his way up to associate head coach on Izzo's staff through the 1998–99 Final Four season. He worked as the recruiting coordinator and was responsible for helping bring Mateen Cleaves (one of the famed "Flintstones" from Flint, MI), Jason Richardson, and Zach Randolph to East Lansing. Crean also helped in the development of another star of the Spartans' Final Four squad, Morris Peterson. Further, Crean called the Spartans' offensive sets during his last year as an assistant in East Lansing.

During each of Crean's seasons at MSU, the Spartans made the NCAA Tournament. The year after he left for Marquette, the Spartans won the national championship and Crean was presented with a commemorative ring. Even though Crean did not have any Division I head coaching experience, he learned his craft at a young age at one of the elite basketball programs in the country, at the feet of one of the nation's best coaches: Tom Izzo.

It helped Crean that he married into a coaching family. Joani's father, Jack, was football coach at Western Kentucky; her brothers Jim (former Chicago Bears quarterback and QB coach for the Oakland Raiders) and John (special teams coach for the Philadelphia Eagles) were also coaches.

As young as Tom Crean was in his first head coaching job (McGuire was just 35 and also had no Division I head coaching experience), it would not have been surprising if he had been intimidated by the McGuire legacy. But Crean instead embraced it, feeling that the legacy of the most successful coach in the school's history was something to build on, rather than something to be feared.

"Obviously, we have a lot of great tradition, but without a doubt we're going to put Marquette's tradition and what has been accomplished here in years past against anyone's. We're not going to be afraid to now try to build on tradition and lay our own footprints. If Marquette University is the house, Al McGuire is the front porch."

When McGuire was asked about the new coach during an interview on John Dodds' "Dodds on Sports" radio show on May 27, 1999, McGuire noted, "He's a great coach, a workaholic. He keeps a good PR and good awareness. And from my knowledge of people who know him, he's a great coach.

"Now, I know he said he was real pleased that all the ballplayers were coming back. But I didn't like it because, you know, they were in last place last year. And he doesn't have scholarships to work with. I think he has one. . . . Once he gets where he can go full-time recruiting and get his own ballplayers, I think they'll start to come. They'll be representative. They'll play hard," was the best endorsement McGuire could give of the players Crean inherited.

"T.C. will get it done, but it won't be until three years," McGuire predicted. "It's impossible to do it any sooner. You're looking at least one, two, three years away. You're in the shallows for two more years. As far as Marquette returning to the glory years, it would have to be once every four years," he added. "I think the crowds will increase. I think Tom Crean is going to capture Marquette fans."

The cupboard was not exactly bare when Crean took over at Marquette. He was inheriting Cordell Henry, Oluoma Nnamaka, John Cliff, Bart Miller, David Diggs, Jon Harris, Greg Clausen, Brian Barone, Brian Wardle, and John Mueller, a nucleus of solid, hardworking players. If ever there was a prototype for a lunch-bucket group of players, this was it. They gave their all on the court and in the classroom. Henry and Wardle were not All-Americas, but they were winners. Henry helped Chicago's Whitney Young High School win the 1998 Illinois Class AA state title, and Wardle's Hinsdale Central reached the state quarterfinals his senior year. Both players had known each other since eighth grade when they played for the Illinois Warriors AAU team. Crean would rely on their floor leadership to help him in his rookie season at Marquette.

Like McGuire, Crean did not waste any time making his presence known in Milwaukee. After getting his basketball camps established,

Crean hit the ground running. He began making contacts with high school and AAU coaches in Wisconsin and Illinois, instituting an "inside-out" recruiting strategy to keep the best players in the state. Once he had established his Wisconsin base, then Crean could move the recruiting radius outward.

The player Crean targeted with his lone scholarship was Wauwatosa East star Scott Merritt, a 6'10" power forward who was considered among the top 50 high school players in the country and the top player in the state of Wisconsin. Merritt also played for Wisconsin's AAU team, the Playground Warriors. Among those schools in the running for Merritt's services included Duke, Kentucky, Illinois, Syracuse, Ohio State, Michigan, Wisconsin, and Pittsburgh.

Crean quickly put together his coaching staff: Tim Buckley (formerly of Ball State), Dwayne Stephens, whom he had brought with him from MSU, and Darrin Horn, whom Crean had coached at Western Kentucky. Then Crean sent his young staff on the road. Crean was armed with a constantly ringing cell phone and an I-PASS transponder so he would not get backed up on Illinois' miles of toll roads, which he traversed looking for diamonds in the rough on the state's basketball courts.

One of the players Crean's staff identified as a prospect early on was a lanky, skinny freshman who was a good shooter, Steve Novak of Brown Deer (Wis.) High School. Novak eventually was courted by the University of Florida, Illinois, Wisconsin, and a number of other schools besides Marquette. When Novak made his campus visit to Marquette, he reportedly hit it off with the players. It seemed like a good fit. "I chose Marquette because there was no program I was interested in that was going to work as hard or win a national championship as quickly," said the 6'10" Novak after he committed.

Crean's staff also liked a high school sophomore at Fond du Lac Goodrich, who, though he still looked like he was in eighth grade, could shoot and exhibited natural leadership skills on the court. Travis Diener was very impressed with Crean.

"He's what you'd call a very persuasive person. . . . He told me Marquette was going back to the top. He made it sound believable," Diener told Tim Layden in the April 7, 2003, issue of *Sports Illustrated*.

St. Louis University (which signed his cousin Drew), Utah, and Wisconsin also recruited the fresh-faced Diener.

Assistant coach Tim Buckley had heard about a forward at Richards High School in Oak Lawn, Illinois, named Dwyane Wade. Buckley saw the 6'5" Wade play during his senior season and alerted Crean that the young man was the real deal. At the time, Wade's high school coach Jack Fitzgerald said that only Illinois State and DePaul had expressed any interest in his player.

During his senior year, Wade scored 89 points in a morning/afternoon holiday basketball tournament. Even after averaging 27 points and 11 rebounds a game his senior year, Wade finished only No. 7 in "Mr. Basketball" voting in the state of Illinois.

In the end, it was Marquette and Crean who showed the most interest in Wade. The only obstacle was that he barely missed qualifying academically for his freshman year of college. Wade had reportedly asked Crean upfront, would he still stick with Wade despite the fact he would be a partial qualifier his freshman year. Crean's answer: an emphatic yes. Dwyane Wade was truly the first test of Crean's loyalty to a player before he even coached at game at Marquette.

The key to each of the three recruits was not only their obvious talent. All three were the stereotypical gym rats, hard workers who stayed after practice and games to work on their free throws and jump shots. These were Crean's kind of guys.

Within two weeks of his hiring, the Creans received more good news: Tom, Joani, and daughter Megan, welcomed a healthy baby boy to their family: Riley.

After the family settled into the Milwaukee area, it was not too long before McGuire left a message on Crean's office answering machine, inviting him out for a day trip to Oconomowoc and the other pools and meadows the old coach liked to frequent. Usually, it is the new coach in town who shows deference to the wizened legend by making the courtesy call. But this time, the Mountain came to Mohammad.

Crean recalled that during the time he spent with the legend, he learned quite a bit about Al McGuire's world, and felt very much at home with him. And the feeling was mutual. McGuire was comfortable enough with the new coach that he began dropping in to Marquette's practices and watching the team learn and grow. When McGuire was broadcasting the team's road games, he would sit on the plane with Wardle and Henry, offering tips and advice on basketball—and life. Al talked, they listened.

McGuire had also reportedly told Crean that Marquette's success that season would depend upon Henry buying into the team concept. McGuire had even critiqued Henry's jump shot after watching the guard play in a pickup game.

The theme for that inaugural season was, "Bring Your Game Face." The team poster featured shots of Marquette students with their faces and bodies painted in blue and gold. The players were posed in the obligatory team shot, and the rookie coach was not wearing the new age spectacles or fine suits that would later define his courtside style.

Crean had a chance to introduce himself to the students when he brought "Midnight Madness" back to Marquette. The last time the basketball program hosted a Midnight Madness was at the Old Gym under Deane. For his Midnight Madness, Crean brought in CBS basketball analyst and longtime McGuire friend, Bill Raftery, as the special guest for the event, which was held in the old Milwaukee Auditorium before a crowd of about 3,400 students.

"The Crean Era began at Marquette on a Monday night, when the Packers and Bears were playing, and I get a call from Crean saying that Wade and Odartey Blankson were signed," recalled Marquette beat reporter Lori Nickel of the *Journal Sentinel.* Wade and Blankson made a conference call to Crean to let him know they were coming together to play at Marquette. "Wade was Crean's George Thompson," Nickel said.

And just like any first-year coach, Crean experienced his share of growing pains. While the pundits predicted a sixth-place finish in the American Division of Conference USA for Marquette, the team finished fourth with an 8-8 record (15-14 overall) during the 1999–2000 campaign. Among the highlights were consecutive wins over top 25 opponents within a four-day span. Marquette won its first road game of the season and first against a ranked road opponent since 1997, when it defeated No. 21 DePaul 69-60 on Jan. 12, 2000. Then it took No. 25 Louisville to overtime at the Bradley Center before defeating the Cardinals 66-64.

Marquette's hard work paid off with a bid to the NIT, where it lost a hard-fought game at Xavier 67-63. Not much of a post-season, but a nice reward for the players' hard work during an up and down campaign.

One of the low lights of Crean's inaugural season was that average attendance slipped under 10,000 per game (9,971) for the first time since the 1966–67 season, McGuire's third in Milwaukee. "It seemed for some games that there were no students at the Bradley Center," recalled Marquette play-by-play announcer Steve "The Homer" True. However, the team played hard and never gave up, no matter how far they were down. Crean also lost one of his assistants after just one year. Tim Buckley returned to Muncie, Indiana, to take over the Ball State basketball program. Tod Kowalczyk of DePere, Wisconsin, was named to the staff as an assistant coach after a three-year stint at Rutgers.

"You're not a success until people get out of their seats," McGuire noted in his 1999 interview on "Dodds On Sports." But first, Crean had to find a way to get people, especially the students, back *in* the seats of the Bradley Center.

Before the 2000 NCAA Tournament, Marquette fans and basketball fans everywhere received bad news. It was announced that McGuire would not be calling any of the games due to a blood disorder. It was unthinkable: the Big Dance without Big Al.

Just as the disease progressed and McGuire was placed in a hospice not far from his home in Brookfield, Crean was welcoming his first recruiting class, which featured such standouts as Merritt, 6'7" forward Odartey Blankson of Hillcrest High School (Country Club, Hills, Illinois), 6'7" Milwaukee native Terry Sanders, who prepped at the Hargrave Military Academy in Virginia, and the darkhorse everyone missed, 6'5" shooting guard Dwyane Wade of Richards High School in Oak Lawn, Illinois. Wade was admitted to Marquette as a partial qualifier, the first ever in school history. He could practice with the team during the 2000–01 season, but could not play in games or travel. McGuire never met Wade or saw him play, but the freshman's blue-chip talent was such that he certainly would have recruited him, even though Wade's parents had grass in front of their home in Robbins, Illinois.

Crean had put together an organized practice and academic schedule for his young players, and no exceptions were made for any player. The practices at the Old Gym were intense, and Wade was starting to make his presence known among his teammates.

"The Old Gym was sticky and hot," recalled Lori Nickel, who covered the team for the Journal Sentinel Crean's first year. "I'm surprised they were not injured. These kids didn't hold anything back."

"There were no out-of-bounds in the Marquette practices," recalled John Baker, photographer for the Marquette basketball fan web site DoddsonSports.com. "The players went after a loose ball until someone came up with it."

There were no jump balls, either. Players were given high grades for taking charges and deflecting passes, statistics that were also kept during games. One of the "football-style" drills Crean brought with him from Michigan State included one for lay-ups that featured assistant coach Dwayne Stephens. As the players approached the basket, Stephens waited with blocking pads on both arms. When a player rose up toward the basket, Stephens gave him a hard forearm shiver to the chest to try to knock him off balance. The idea was to get the players used to finishing the play even while getting a hard foul. Crean wanted his players to get tough, when the going got tough.

"Tom Crean's practices run for three or more hours," noted Todd Rosiak, who began covering the team for the *Journal Sentinel* during the 2002–03 season. "They are very intense, almost brutal. The practices are so defensive oriented, so hustle oriented, so toughness oriented. All 10 guys are expected to go after the ball. Three or four guys would dive into doors or the bleachers. It was like a free-for-all scrum on the floor. The entire team would form a circle around the players, cheering on the guys going for the ball."

"During one practice," Rosiak continued, "Wade and Robert Jackson were wrestling for the ball for two minutes, when Wade came out of the pile with the ball. He took two steps and did a reverse dunk and let out a roar as he hung onto the rim."

"It was a war for some of those drills, crashing and diving," Nickel added. "You would see bodies flying. When you see that in practices, you would not be surprised to see it in games. He [Crean] actually brought that alive in a practice setting.

"Generally speaking, practices were some of the most intense I'd ever seen. I would sit there and wait that I would be writing that so and so would blow out a knee diving after the ball."

McGuire's practices were equally intense, so intense that fisticuffs would break out among the players. When asked if this were the case with Crean's workouts, Nickel said, "I'm sure it happened a couple of times, but there's no energy left to take it out on teammates after a Crean practice." Nickel added that some of the players admitted off the record that Crean was pushing them too hard in practice.

"Especially players who weren't used to that. Even a couple of Deane's players wondered. I seem to remember talking to Crean about it. He did make adjustments, but he believed that top athletes who went to the Final Four are going to want to practice like that all year round. He knew how long and how hard to push them."

In another drill, Crean lined the players up along the baseline, placing the ball in a different place each time. He would blow his whistle and players would have to get the ball. Those who came up with the ball could leave the baseline; those who did not had to go back in line again, until they finally came up with the ball. For rebounding drills, players would get a point for a defensive rebound and two points for an offensive rebound. Whoever lost had to run the suicide drills. "What kind of defender you were and how tough you were determined playing time," Rosiak noted.

"When a player took a charge in a practice drill or a game," continued Rosiak, the other players would rush up and slap him on the butt," which helped build a one for all, all for one camaraderie on the squad.

During the early practices of the 2000–01 campaign, it was not unusual for some of the veteran players to just sit back and marvel at Wade's athletic ability and talent. It seemed as if the other players were waiting for him to make something happen, which irked the freshman. Word started to spread about Wade's athleticism, explosiveness, quickness, and above-the-rim play. Soon, NBA scouts started showing up at Marquette practices. Wade also role-played the opposing team's star player in workouts to help the team prepare for its games.

Assistant Tod Kowalczyk was assigned to work with Wade, coming up with drills to help improve the young man's game and preparing him for the next season. When the team bus was preparing to leave, Wade would go to the bus and see his teammates off. After the bus left, a glum Wade with school backpack slung over his shoulder, would head off to the library for some study.

Later, Wade would watch the team's game on TV back at Humphrey Hall and afterward critique his teammates' performance via cell phone, talking to each of the players. This was Crean's way of making Wade feel a more integral part of the team as the young man waited his turn to join the squad the following season. He earned a 3.0 grade point average his freshman season, earning his playing eligibility for the next campaign.

As Wade was quietly making a name for himself behind closed doors, Crean continued to make regular pilgrimages to the dying legend in Brookfield. As a result of these private sessions, both men grew to know and respect each other in the short time they had together. It would be only 18 months.

"He meant so much to me in such a short period of time, because he took an interest in me and knew that I was a willing participant and trying to learn. And I learned so much. But I really learned a great deal of why he was so successful was the way he treated people and the way he touched them. Whether they knew him five minutes or fifty years, it didn't make any difference," reflected Crean, the new-age coach with the old-school ethic.

Most of the 3,800 students who attended the second Midnight Madness under the Crean Administration received their official gold T-shirts to be worn at the Bradley Center. All were eager to see Wade first-hand, as they filed into the US Cellular Arena. The special guest for Midnight Madness II was ESPN analyst Jay Bilas, a friend of Crean and of the Marquette program.

At this time, Marquette was planning a new basketball practice facility on campus to help Crean in his recruiting efforts and to reinvigorate the basketball program. This was something to look forward to, along with higher hopes for Crean's second season.

The university had asked McGuire and his family for permission to name the facility for him. After lengthy consultations with family members and Marquette, McGuire agreed to have it named the Alfred E.

McGuire Center. On Oct. 16, 2000, Marquette made the announcement, and later that day, James H. and Virginia Wheeler, longtime Marquette supporters, donated a $2 million challenge gift toward the project. This came on the heels of a $7 million anonymous donation.

"We had to work very hard to get Al to allow us to use his name on the facility," recalled Marquette President Wild. "Al was very reluctant to do it. [But once] he saw how important the project was, he was very supportive. It took Allie and his siblings to convince Al he should do this. I do think people liked the idea that this facility would be named for him."

The state-of-the-art center would include a 5,000-seat arena for the women's basketball team, practice courts for the men's and women's teams and women's volleyball squad, the Marquette Sports Hall of Fame, an academic center, locker rooms, and a weight-training facility, all at a cost of $31 million.

In the midst of all these developments, the Golden Eagles prepared for their opening-round game of the Preseason NIT against South Alabama. Earlier in the week, it had been erroneously reported by a Milwaukee area radio station that Al McGuire had died. Before the game, a taped address from McGuire was played at the Bradley Center in which he insisted that the rumors of his passing had been "greatly exaggerated," and that he was ice fishing in northern Wisconsin with Elvis, which drew howls of laughter from the crowd.

Next up at the Bradley Center was UMASS, a game that was broadcast on ESPN2. The nip-and-tuck game ended with Marquette taking a 68-64 decision. And after the game, Coach Crean began high-fiving those in the student section, showing his appreciation for their support. Fans had not seen that kind of enthusiasm from a Marquette head coach in some time.

After winning three in a row, Marquette lost to instate rival Wisconsin for the third straight year. The Badgers, under popular coach Dick Bennett, would advance to the Final Four later that season for only the second time in school history.

A pattern was starting to develop for this Marquette team. It would win one, lose one; win one, lose two. It followed that way for the rest of the season. And while the results were uneven, Crean stuck with his rugged regimen for practice and games.

"Coach Crean is the hardest-working coach whom I have ever met," noted Wardle. "He is always working on ways to make the team better. He leads by example—when you see how hard he works, and the dedication that he has, it makes you want to work hard and go the extra mile."

Crean was also winning high marks from his peers and the media for his game preparation, especially the number of different offensive sets he employed during games. For road games, Crean tried to get his players into practice earlier so they could take as much time as needed to work on the sets.

Marquette's first game of the new millennium was at DePaul, Jan. 6, 2001. Before the game, Crean had his team at the Allstate Arena early for practice. That week the team had come off a tough 61-60 loss at Dayton and a morning practice was scheduled for the next day. The players had very little sleep but made it to practice, which Crean recalled was one of the best of the season.

Watching the Jan. 6 pre-game workout with great interest was then DePaul play-by-play announcer Dan Bernstein.

"I was watching the team practice and noted all of the different sets Crean was having these guys go through. I got out a note pad and just started writing these sets down.

"After Marquette left the floor, I went to one of the DePaul assistants and asked him, 'Do you guys do this set?' He said, 'no.' 'Do you guys do this set?' He said, 'no.' I was just very impressed by his game preparation," noted Bernstein, a morning sports talk radio host on Chicago's WSCR-AM, "The Score." Marquette won the game in impressive fashion, 69-49, before DePaul's largest home crowd of the season—13,306—many of whom were Marquette fans. As Marquette pulled away in the second half, the strains of WE ARE MARQUETTE could be heard echoing louder throughout the Allstate Arena.

Marquette's schedule had improved since Crean's first season, with UMASS, Xavier, and Minnesota added for the 2000–01 campaign. But the sternest test would come on Jan. 13, 2001, at Chapel Hill. Crean scheduled a game with the University of North Carolina, but could get no return match in Milwaukee. Marquette lost by 30 to Matt Doherty's No. 9 ranked University of North Carolina Tar Heels, 84-54.

Marquette had just come off an emotional 47-44 win at home over Cincinnati earlier in the week, in which the team used a slowdown game to tame Bob Huggins' Bearcats. Before ABC's broadcast of the MU-UNC game, pregame show host Digger Phelps said Marquette would have to use a similar game plan against UNC in order to have a chance to win.

Unfortunately, that game plan did not work against the Tar Heels, but it was not an embarrassing loss, because the Golden Eagles never gave up and continued to play hard until the end. The team patiently ran its offensive sets, working for good shots. Defensively, Marquette stayed within its game plan, and toward the end of the game the players still kept their arms upraised and continued to work. It was just a case of Marquette running into a quicker, taller, deeper, more talented, and more experienced team. MU was not intimidated, though, and did not back down. Noted ABC-TV analyst Brad Daugherty, "If they can get that one player that can come in and be explosive offensively for them, they're gonna be a better basketball team because they have the defensive thing going."

At that juncture, the game was a measuring stick for the basketball program. The result showed Crean and his players just how far they had to go in order to be able to play with the best teams in the country. There was reason for optimism, however. As the camera panned the long faces of the Marquette players on the bench, ABC's Brad Nessler noted, "There'll be brighter times, because you can't play as hard as they've played and have the fruits of your efforts go unrewarded." "I'll tell you, this Marquette basketball program with Tom Crean in charge is going to go through the roof. He's an excellent basketball coach and has brought a lot of enthusiasm to the game," predicted Daugherty, who praised freshmen Scott Merritt and Odartey Blankson for the flashes of brilliance they showed in the losing cause.

The nation also had a chance to see Crean's coaching style. During the game, he used just about every inch of the coaching box. Pacing back and forth in front of the Marquette bench, Crean never used his seat the entire game. Pointing instructions, pacing, clapping, and working the referees at the Dean Smith Center, Crean crowded the box only so far, before going back inside. The closest he ever did get to sitting down was a crouch, and then down to one knee. Even McGuire, who paced with the best of coaches, would sit down every now and then. Not Crean. As the outcome of the Carolina game was becoming painfully clear, his arms were folded and right at the end his chin was resting in his hand. The frustration on Crean's face was palpable as he realized there was nothing else that he could do to help his team win that day.

As the season wore on, Crean continued to throw himself whole-heartedly into promoting the fundraising events and activities for the Alfred E. McGuire Center. Crean made the commitment not only to Marquette but to Coach McGuire, whom he would see for the last time on Tuesday afternoon, Jan. 23, 2001. After that meeting, Crean reportedly pulled his car over to the side of the road and wept. The parallels of building the McGuire Center and the Marquette basketball program were more appropriate than ironic. In order to build on a legacy, Crean and the university would have to build a complex that would secure Marquette's basketball future.

Crean and his players embraced the McGuire legacy. However, the torch had not yet been passed from the old coach to the new, until McGuire's death on Friday morning, Jan. 26, 2001, after a long bout with leukemia. The next afternoon, a large crowd filed into the Bradley Center to honor McGuire. A large black and white photo of the late coach loomed from above on the arena's Jumbotron, and a long moment of silence turned into a deafening roar. The Marquette players fed on the emotion of the moment and took apart Tulane, 82-57.

The following Monday evening, Jan. 29, the Gesu Church was packed for McGuire's funeral. Crean and his players were there to pay their final respects on the cold, rainy night in Milwaukee, nearly 24 years after McGuire's triumphant rainy night in Georgia.

At the end of the funeral, as the Marquette players escorted the coffin of the Last Warrior out of Gesu and Milwaukee, they were solemn, dignified, and respectful. They displayed great Marquette pride. For those who were there, it was an emotional and magical night.

It was at that moment, when the players experienced how special Al McGuire had been to his former players assembled on the altar, to the Marquette extended family, and to the City of Milwaukee, that they understood and appreciated the power of his legacy. They got it, even though none of them had been born when Marquette last won a national championship.

And it was at that moment that the torch was passed to them and their young coach—albeit a generation removed from the glory days presided over by McGuire.

But somehow Crean already understood the legacy he was inheriting. He probably understood it when he was an 11-year-old watching Al's Warriors win the national championship back in 1977. He accepted the legacy's weight and its awesome responsibility. And as a young coach he not only bought into it, but wove the McGuire thread into his personal coaching tapestry.

The next night, Tuesday evening, Jan. 30, the team hosted conference opponent Southern Mississippi at the Bradley Center. But the Marquette players were too spent from riding the emotional roller coaster of the previous week and lost 78-65. The events of the previous week had obviously taken their toll on the young team.

In order to keep the late coach as a constant reminder, Crean had black circular patches with the name AL in white letters sewn above the left breast of the players' jerseys. The patches were debuted on "Fill the Corners for Al Night" during a Feb. 22, 2001, ESPN game against DePaul. While the corners of the Bradley Center were not filled that night, more than 17,000 fans braved the bitter cold to see the court renamed the "Al McGuire Court." There were swatches of gold in the lower level of the student section, but no solid gold there or anywhere else in the arena. The Golden Eagles were led in their 82-64 win by Henry (22 points) and Wardle (21), who scored 20 or more for the twelfth time that season, as well as a double-double from Blankson (14 points, 11 rebounds).

As with McGuire and his players, Crean was close enough in age to understand his young players and they him. While at the same time, Crean was old enough for them to respect him. The young players and young coach would somehow grow the program together.

Crean also took a page out of the McGuire notebook by finding ways to bring the students back to the Bradley Center, as well as the longtime fans who became disaffected by the program's recent trend toward mediocrity. He was determined to create a home-court advantage at the arena, and he looked for ways to sell the team and the program to students and the community. Crean tried to market the team to each class at the university after he arrived in Milwaukee. His personal pitch received the most enthusiastic response from the freshmen. As a result, Crean decided to cultivate each incoming freshman class, so that by the time each of those classes became seniors the student section would be a loud, proud Marquette crowd. Perfect for televised games. This was Crean's version of McGuire's "Senior Star" system.

Crean offered coffee and donut breakfasts to the students as well as pizza parties on campus, where he answered students' questions about the team, schedule, and whether the Golden Eagles would make the NCAA Tournament. After the season, he sponsored free cookouts outside the university's Memorial Union as a "thank-you" to the students who had purchased "Fanatic Packages," which included season tickets and free gold T-shirts. Crean invited special guests to the cookouts, including ESPN analyst Jay Bilas. The first season the T-shirts were blue, but because they did not show up well enough on television, Crean insisted on gold. McGuire took a similar interest in not only how the team's uniforms looked on television, but the cheerleaders' uniforms as well. Both coaches understood the power of television and the entertainment aspect of the game. Crean also used e-mail reminders before big games to make sure the students and their friends made it to the games.

After the Bradley Center was darkened before tip-off, the image of a golden eagle crashing through a glass backboard preceded a short video of the team, which was spliced with footage of McGuire and his championship season to remind the fans of the importance of tradition and how Crean's young charges were going to carry it on. The player introductions were also hip-hopped with music the players AND young students could relate to. U2's "Where The Streets Have No Name," a favorite of the team, was used to bring the players onto the floor. In addition, Music In Motion was hired to provide music for the games and time-outs, making the game an entertainment event. "What you hear is mostly ballpark music," commented photographer John Baker, who generally has a courtside seat for the pregame hoopla. And as the players come onto the floor, giant inflatable dancers gyrate to the music, which featured everything from Zombie Nation to Ray Charles.

But it worked both ways. While Crean wanted the students to take ownership of the team, he also wanted the players to take their share of ownership and be ambassadors for the team and the university. Crean reminded them to be polite to other students, make eye contact when they talked to them, and to say "hello" on campus. Additionally, players made regular telephone calls to season ticket holders and alumni to personally thank them for their support. Crean's reach-out-and-touch someone philosophy was designed to bring the team closer to the fans by showing appreciation for their support, which did not go unnoticed by many alums.

"Tom Crean is an unusual combination of old-school and new-school coaches. He blends the youthful enthusiasm and extraordinary player relationships he possesses with the work ethic and individual responsibility and accountability of the early-day coaches," explained CBS' Raftery.

While Marquette swept both Cincinnati and DePaul during the 2000–2001 campaign, it lost a triple-overtime thriller to Louisville on Senior Night, in the last game Denny Crum would coach for the Cardinals in Milwaukee. The loss (believed to be the only triple-overtime game in Marquette history) seemed to deflate the team, and it went on to lose three of its last four games to finish Crean's second season at 15-14 (9-7 in the American Division of Conference USA—good enough for third place, but better than the fifth-place preseason prediction). Its imbalance could be seen in the fact that the Golden Eagles were the best free-throw shooting team and yet the worst rebounding team in Conference USA.

There would be no post-season, but there were honors for some of the players, including senior Brian Wardle, who earned C-USA First Team honors, a first for a Marquette player; junior Cordell Henry was named Third Team; and Odartey Blankson made the All-Freshman team. But most important, the team excelled in the classroom, earning the highest grade-point average in the conference for the third straight season. That was the main reason the university decided to charter Midwest Airlines for the team's road trips, so that the players could fly home after games to attend classes the next day.

Crean was also getting national recognition for his coaching prowess. He was named a court coach for USA Basketball's National Team Trials in Colorado Springs. However, as well as his team was praised for its never-say-die attitude, some were beginning to question whether Crean was driving the team too hard toward the end of the season. While he was getting a reputation as a good recruiter, some of his coaching and practice decisions were being questioned. Just as with McGuire after his second season, when the team finished 14-12, fans and media were wondering if Crean could get the job done.

"There were muted mutterings from some fans in his second year," recalled President Wild. "But people quickly realized it would take time. It is not good for a university president to micromanage athletics or second-guess the people in charge."

"This year we've tried to be known as a team that really understands it's a blue-collar game," Crean told ABC in an interview taped before the North Carolina game. "Rebounding on both ends is crucial for us. And even as we continue to improve, which I think we will over the next few years, we're not going to win games and substantial games without that mentality, especially on the defensive end.

"Because we're not a team that can find easy baskets. We don't have a lot of people who can find a shot on their own at the end of the shot clock. We've got to rely on each other. We've got to rely on our ability to defend and rebound." ∎

CHAPTER TWO:
LEARNING TO FLY

After two years of growing pains and limited expectations, year three of the Crean Era was about to kick off. Attendance had shot up to 11,360 per game the previous season, and Crean was seeing his blueprint for success slowly begin to take shape. The slogan for the 2001–02 season was "Ready to Fly," but Crean was not sure yet just how high this group of Golden Eagles could soar.

"Obviously, when you take over a new program, especially one that had been struggling, it is a situation where it is going to take time to develop your plan of attack in all areas. The program needed a lot of restructuring and reshaping, and I think that we are on the road to doing that.

"We'll now see the transitional phase of a lot of youth in this program, but I think in due time that we will see the benefits of it," Crean predicted.

"Tom has gone through the highs and lows of any new coach during his first two years. But now with his people and system in place, combined with the excellent recruiting, the future is bright for Marquette basketball," predicted George Thompson.

Marquette was picked to reprise its third place finish in the American Division of C-USA, and nobody was predicting NCAA Tournament for Golden Eagles. In fact, they were not ranked in any preseason basketball publications or polls. The verdict on the team and its young coach was still out as far as the national media were concerned. The team was returning three starters and five of its top six scorers, accounting for 62.5 percent of its scoring and 74.5 percent of its rebounding. But Marquette was losing Wardle's 18.8 points per game and leadership to graduation.

"With the loss of Brian, it will be important that our scoring be spread out and that we have more balance," commented Crean. "I think that some of our players will step to the forefront and become go-to players, but we do not have that player like Brian that you are going to look to night-in and night-out to make things happen. We do have a group of players who I believe can develop into those type players."

While the pundits' expectations were low, fans were especially excited because the coming campaign would be their chance to see what they had been hearing all about for over a year: Dwyane Wade. Fans were optimistic that Wade could be that go-to player to whom Crean was referring. Wade, a sophomore, was probably the best Marquette player since Glenn "Doc" Rivers. Many fans were thinking out loud that the team could be "Goin' Uptown," like McGuire's third team which won 21 games and advanced to the NIT Finals in 1967.

Crean obviously knew what he had in Wade, but tried to downplay whatever contribution he might make that season, simply because it was his first full year of collegiate competition. He also did not want to get fans' hopes up too high.

"My biggest concern with Dwyane is that we all have to be patient enough to allow him to develop and gain experience."

But Wade was not the only bright light who would be helping MU that season. Marquette had nice senior leadership in guards Henry (5'10") and David Diggs (6'4") and 6'7" forwards Oluoma Nnamka of Uppsala, Sweden, and Jon Harris of Edwardsville, Illinois. Sophomore Scott Merritt, who would play center, was coming along nicely, even though he was not playing his natural No. 4 position. Sophomores Odartey Blankson, 6'7", and Terry Sanders, 6'8", rounded out the cast. Sanders, who had won two state championships at Milwaukee Vincent High School before heading to the Hargrave Military Academy in Virginia, lost most of his freshman year due to a bout of mononucleosis.

Marquette welcomed a top-30 recruiting class that included highly regarded 6' point guard Travis Diener of Fond du Lac, a fourth-team

Parade Magazine All-American; Chicago-area recruits 6'5" guard/forward Ron Howard from Whitney Young High School, forwards 6'7" Todd Townsend of New Trier High School, and 6'5" Kevin Menard of Lincoln-Way; and Mississippi State transfer and Milwaukee native, 6'10" center Robert Jackson, who would have to sit out the season under NCAA transfer rules but could practice with the team. This was one of the best recruiting classes Marquette had had in some time. Some questioned why Crean would take a player like Jackson, who had only one year of eligibility remaining. But Crean needed an "aircraft carrier" at the center position, and also felt the experienced Jackson could help Merritt become a better player.

In order to get the talented freshmen quickly acclimated to his practice and academic regimen, Crean asked them to come to Milwaukee during the summer. The orientation would include not just basketball, weight training, and workouts, but also some classes. He wanted them to get a jump-start on the academic year and get to know their teammates.

Crean also added some NBA experience to his staff, with the hiring of special assistant Trey Schwab. A former advance scout and college scout for the Minnesota Timberwolves, Schwab's expertise extended to technology, especially video. He had also worked as a video coordinator for the T-Wolves.

As the school year began, expectations were high and fans were looking ahead to what they hoped would be an exciting season. Unfortunately, reality intruded on those dreams and aspirations in the early morning of Sept. 11, 2001, as students were heading to their classes. Terrorist highjackers commandeered planes that were flown into the twin towers of New York's World Trade Center and the Pentagon. A fourth plane crashed into the countryside outside of Pittsburgh, PA.

When 9-11 took place, senior and third generation Marquette student Jaci Pabst of Grand Rapids, Michigan, was in a lab. "I went back to the dorm and saw everything on TV. I was in total shock."

"It was the strangest thing I've ever experienced," said Pabst, who was living in Carpenter Hall at the time. "I wasn't even aware that it had happened. Classes were canceled that afternoon," she recalled. "I had never heard the city so quiet. It was an eerie silence."

The cruel and tragic interruption of life hit the Marquette community and all others around the country very hard. There were a number of people in the Marquette extended family who were lost in the tragedy, which served as a harsh reminder of the fleeting nature of life, and helped bring the entire Marquette family together before many students were settled into their first semester of college life.

"There was a lot of disbelief and fear on campus," Pabst continued. "It [9-11] brought about a lot more spirituality because of all the memorials and prayer services and masses.

"Thousands of people gathered in front of West Towne Square near the Alumni Memorial Union. Father Wild addressed the crowd. I couldn't believe how quiet it was. Total silence. It was so weird standing with thousands of others and everyone was so quiet. It pulled people together."

"Talking to some of the [ROTC] officers who had lost good friends at the Pentagon, it was so shocking," recalled Marquette President Rev. Wild. "We had three alums die. Students had relatives, a lot of linkage, a lot of feeling and emotional uncertainty it created. It brought people more in touch. A drawing together. It was the spector of vulnerability for our country."

It hit home especially with freshman Travis Diener, whose cousin Derek was stationed at Ft. Hood, not knowing where Derek would be sent. While Travis was getting a chance to play basketball and get an education in the relative safety of a college campus, his cousin would be placed in harm's way every day.

Later that month, Diener's family also mourned the loss of Travis's half brother, Dan, who had died suddenly. Dan was older than Travis and also played basketball at their alma mater, Fond du Lac Goodrich High School. In solidarity with Travis, the Marquette team, led by Coach Crean and team Chaplain Rev. William Kelly, attended the funeral. The extended Marquette family came through for the Dieners, which "meant a lot to the family," according to Jim Ganzer, a longtime Marquette fan and season ticket holder since 1991.

By the time the United States had its troops on the ground in Afghanistan, sports teams—collegiate and professional—all across the country showed their solidarity with the troops by wearing the American

Flag on their jerseys. Marquette followed suit just before the 2001–02 season, getting Old Glory sewn onto the front of its uniforms.

Even with all of the sobering "real world" news, the university did have some good news to announce. As of mid-October, Marquette University had raised approximately $18 million in cash and pledges toward the $31 million McGuire Center. The news jump-started Midnight Madness III at the Milwaukee Arena, where the students were dressed in their trademark gold T-shirts, psyched for the upcoming campaign. They came to see Dwyane Wade, who strutted his stuff to win the Slam Dunk Contest. There was also quite a buzz about who the evening's "special guest" was going to be. Halfway through the evening's festivities, former heavyweight boxing champ and grill spokesman George Foreman sauntered into the Arena, as he prepared to knock out emcee Steve "The Homer" True, much to the delight of the cheering students. It was a brief but memorable appearance that raised the eyebrows of some of the media in attendance. It showed that Marquette was very serious about taking the program big time.

"With Wade, all of a sudden, the guy was a draw," recalled Lori Nickel. "And nobody knew about him but Marquette fans. They're dying to watch him play."

"I went to Indiana, and major programs like Indiana and Duke always had Midnight Madness," noted Nickel. "I had never seen Marquette act like a big-time program. You felt this change, even though they hadn't won yet. You'd see alums who worked in suits all day show up at Midnight Madness. This coach is starting this. It did strike me that it started with the Midnight Madness, the image Crean created."

Watching this particular group of players that night, it was pretty clear these guys liked each other. There was good-natured ribbing and lots of pats on the back. There was some kind of esprit de corps happening, with an all-for-one, one-for-all attitude permeating the group.

Marquette was getting ready to continue its journey toward respectability that season, but a number of things had to happen in order for the program to take that next step. In Crean's first two years, the team showed a toughness, a resiliency, a willingness to work hard and get the occasional upset over a ranked opponent. But the team played inconsistently, which was evident in the identical 15-14 records. The team also had losing road records those first two seasons (3-8 and 4-7). However, the team did make improvements in Conference USA play over the previous season in field-goal percentage (39% to 44%), scoring offense (62.8 ppg to 69 ppg), and free-throw percentage (68% to 74%).

One man who was not worried about where Tom Crean would take Marquette, however, was Michigan State head coach Tom Izzo.

"Watching the progress of the Marquette program the past two years just confirms what I have known all along about Tom Crean. That his tireless work ethic, whether it comes to recruiting, game preparation, or individual instruction, is what sets him apart from many and evident in how his teams play. He definitely has a plan for how to achieve success for the Marquette program and that promises to bring excitement to its fans for years to come."

In order to take the next step, Marquette also had to show it could come from behind and win on the road, protect its home-court advantage, be good enough to overcome injuries and bad calls, and win a regular season conference championship, which Marquette had not accomplished since the 1993–94 season when O'Neill's Warriors won the Great Midwest Conference. But they also needed a go-to player, somebody who would want the ball at crunch time. A player who would take the fans out of their seats and carry the team on his shoulders if need be.

Once the season began, Marquette had found that player in Wade. The sophomore with the senior cut exploded out of the box in wins over Loyola and Bo Ellis' Chicago State Cougars. His stat-sheet-stuffer reputation was growing quickly. Against Loyola, Wade's line included 21 points, nine rebounds, five assists, two blocked shots, and three steals. Against Chicago State: 19 points, 14 rebounds, six assists, and three steals.

During one early-season home game, as Wade was once again filling his stat sheet, Marquette radio analyst George Thompson was chatting with Steve "The Homer" True about how much longer Thompson's all-time scoring record of 1,773 points might last. "I'm toast, Homer," Thompson said of his record, as he watched Wade take the opposing team apart at both ends of the floor with his lightning-quick first step, leaping ability, and hustle. Even at that early stage, Wade seemed to have an endless repertoire of moves. As word spread about his talent, fans continued to return to the Bradley Center, in case they might miss something.

Marquette's journey next took the team to Anchorage to play in the Great Alaska Shootout. Other teams in the GAS included perennial NCAA teams Tennessee, Gonzaga, Texas, St. John's, and No. 11-ranked Indiana. Marquette was not the favorite, but certainly played like one.

Wade, a budding superstar, burst onto the scene in Anchorage. He started out by torching Tennessee for 30 points, eight rebounds, seven assists, five steals, and a blocked shot in Marquette's opening round 85-74 win. Next up was Mike Davis' Indiana Hoosiers. Marquette ice-picked an impressive defensive victory, 50-49, with Wade getting 21 points, eight rebounds, one assist, two blocked shots, and a steal. It was Wade's put-back with time running out that sealed the win. Hoosier All-America Jared Jeffries was held to eight points.

In the championship game against Gonzaga, while Wade's performance (13 points, seven rebounds, five assists, two blocked shots and a steal) was worthy of tournament MVP honors, it was senior David Diggs' 5-for-5 three-point shooting that won the game 72-63. Freshman guard Travis Diener made waves with his cool long-range shooting. He scored 14 points, hitting four of eight from three-point range. Diener's cool under pressure earned him the nickname "Teenage Assassin" from Steve "The Homer" True. Gonzaga's All-Everything Dan Dickau was held to just 10 points by Henry.

Winning three games in four days a long way from home, Marquette's players really came together as a team. One of the memorable moments afterward was of a smiling Crean holding aloft the championship trophy. It was the first time in school history that Marquette had won such a pre-season tournament, and it put the team on the national basketball map. The GAS championship showed the nation that the team was for real, and made the nation sit up and take notice of Dwyane Wade for more than just the unusual spelling of his first name. Marquette cracked AP's top 25 poll, coming in at No. 23, and began its steady ascent up the charts. Winning that championship started a swell of momentum that carried the team on a wonderful, unexpected ride. Wade was the only Marquette player named to the GAS all-tournament team.

While no one expected this Marquette team to go to the Final Four that season or anytime soon, the GAS was a stepping stone for the team (and the program), and it showed that it could beat perennial NCAA contenders on a neutral floor. In fact, the Indiana team Marquette defeated would eventually lose to Maryland in the 2002 NCAA Championship game.

Marquette returned triumphantly from Anchorage for its annual Blue & Gold holiday tournament in the Bradley Center. It defeated Texas Southern 76-40 and Sam Houston State 77-58 to win its third straight Classic, and extended its early season record to 6-0. Wade then led four MU players in double figures with 17 points in an easy 73-51 win over Dayton.

"The Dayton game is when the gold T-shirts were really becoming prominent in the student section," recalled Shawn Killian, a 2003 Marquette graduate from Des Plaines, Illinois. "That was the first game where attendance really picked up. There was a lot of gold. It [student section] was fuller than previous games and previous years."

Wins number nine and 10 came over Fordham and Arkansas–Pine Bluff at the Bradley Center, with Wade leading four and six players, respectively, in double figures. Crean and Schwab took advantage of the 11 days between the Fordham and Arkansas games to make a recruiting trip. During their time away from Milwaukee, they both contracted pneumonia. Schwab stayed with the Creans while he recuperated. Coach Crean's health slowly started to improve before the Wisconsin game, but he was forced to miss a practice, which was unbelievable, according to Lori Nickel, who was the team's beat reporter for Crean's first three years. However, Schwab did not improve.

His condition worsened, precipitating a move to the hospital where, on Dec. 19, Schwab was diagnosed with a serious lung disease—idiopathic pulmonary fibrosis. IPF attacks the air sacs in the lungs and limits the body's ability to process oxygen. The doctors treating Schwab told him he had a 40 percent chance of living three years with the disease.

The 38-year-old assistant was put on a 10-medication-a-day regimen, which included an experimental drug, Actimmune. Schwab also worked out on a stationary bike and treadmill, losing a hundred pounds. During the course of his treatment he underwent six surgeries, including the removal of his gallbladder. Through all of this Schwab never missed a game and became an inspiration to Coach Crean and the team.

Marquette next brought a 10-game winning streak and No. 14 ranking to Madison to play bitter instate rival Wisconsin at the Kohl Center.

Wade, Blankson, and Townsend were all nursing nagging injuries that were carryovers from Alaska and the subsequent games. Wade's left knee was bothering him. Blankson had a stress fracture in one of his feet, and Townsend was suffering from tendonitis in his achilles tendons. That afternoon the Golden Eagles had no answer for Kirk Penney's 33 points as the Badgers won 86-73. It was Marquette's fourth straight loss to Wisconsin. Crean still had not beaten the Badgers, who were now coached by Bo Ryan. It was Marquette's first road loss, and now it was headed to Winston-Salem, North Carolina, to play Wake Forest.

The Demon Deacons (ranked No. 25 in the country) were the second ranked team Marquette played in the season's early going. The Golden Eagles had been beaten badly at Chapel Hill the year before, and they were heading down Tobacco Road once again to face another very good ACC opponent on its home floor.

Wake Forest had an experienced team, with five seniors and junior All-America forward Josh Howard. Marquette had a tough time with the Deacons' inside game that afternoon. In fact, Wake blocked eight shots. Down by 13 at the half and as many as 19 points, Marquette came roaring all the way back behind Dwyane Wade's 22 points, (the only Marquette player in double figures) as the team lost by five, 64-59. Unfortunately, Henry was not on the floor for the final few minutes of the game, having played just 22 minutes and scored six points. While the Golden Eagles lost, it showed for the first time under Crean that they could come back from a big deficit on the road and make a game of it in a hostile arena.

In its storied history, Marquette had never beaten ANY North Carolina team in the Tar Heel State. In fact, the only time Marquette ever won a game in the state was during the 1974 Final Four, when it defeated Kansas 64-51 in Greensboro to advance to the NCAA Finals against North Carolina State. McGuire's Warriors defeated three teams from North Carolina during its '77 championship run: Wake Forest, UNC–Charlotte, and North Carolina, but all on neutral courts. Halton Arena, home of the UNC–Charlotte 49ers, has been a house of horrors for Marquette teams over the years. The skein continued during the 2001–02 campaign, when the Golden Eagles lost their Conference USA opener in Charlotte, 76-68. Marquette had four players in double figures, led by Nnamaka (14) and Wade (12), but had no answer for sharp-shooting Jobey Thomas' 26 points. Once again, Marquette could not solve the Charlotte jinx.

"After losing at Charlotte, there was a dip [in attendance]," recalled Killian, "but once we started winning again, attendance picked up. That's when you saw more students in the upper deck, and not just the first row of seats."

Marquette just picked itself up and started another streak, this time winning 12 straight conference games, which was another first for Marquette. The streak started at Louisville's Freedom Hall before 19,607 crazed Cardinals' fans. Marquette started the game on a 19-0 run, and held on to win the hard-fought game against the Cardinals, 75-71. During the pregame coach's show, Cardinals radio analyst Bob Valvano asked one of Rick Pitino's assistant coaches if the team was prepared for Tom Crean's numerous sets.

"That depends on whether you're talking about the 75 sets he uses in transition, the 75 sets off a turnover on the fast break, or the 75 sets he uses in his half-court offense." Marquette turned the ball over 20 times, but still managed to win with balanced scoring. Marquette had four players in double figures, led by Wade's 15 points and eight rebounds, and Blankson's double-double (12 points, 14 rebounds).

On Jan. 12, 2002, Marquette ice-picked a 61-53 win over St. Louis during the 25th anniversary celebration of the school's national championship. A video of Al McGuire was played during halftime, and Hank Raymonds presented all of the '77 Championship players (except Bernard Toone) to the crowd of 13,542. Wade scored just seven points that night, his lowest scoring output as a collegian. The Billikens were somehow able to keep him under wraps, unlike any other team that played Marquette. Blankson picked up the slack that night, scoring a career-high 23 points.

The Dwyane Wade Traveling Show's next stop was Jan. 19, 2002, for a matinee at DePaul. The game was Wade's first visit home as a collegian, and he made the visit a memorable one. That very afternoon Michael Jordan returned to the United Center, this time as an opponent, wearing the uniform of the Washington Wizards. While the United Center was sold out, some 8,254 saw the real show at the Allstate Arena. Wade scored a career-high 35 points, added nine rebounds, six steals, three assists, and three blocked shots. His backcourt mate Henry—who was never offered a scholarship by DePaul—added 27 points as Marquette won 87-68 for its fourth straight win over DePaul. It pushed Marquette's record to 4-1 in conference and 15-3 overall. The 15 wins matched the total number of wins Crean had in each of his first two seasons in Milwaukee, and there were still 14 games left in the season.

The game marked DePaul's largest home crowd that season, but at least half the crowd was comprised of gold-clad Marquette fans, a number of whom were wearing cheese-head wedges. Wade punctuated his personal-best performance when Henry set him up for an acrobatic alley-oop reverse jam, which brought oohs and aahs throughout the Allstate Arena, as well as the loud, continuous chant of WE ARE MARQUETTE. Wade cut his finger on the play, which landed him on the bench with just under five minutes left in the game so as not to do any more damage to himself or DePaul, which had yet to win a conference game. Oh, and Michael Jordan scored a pedestrian 16 points in his game against the Bulls. Those who were at the Allstate Arena, though, knew they witnessed something special.

The following week, a frustrated Gene Sullivan, the late DePaul athletic director and radio analyst, while promoting an upcoming DePaul-Marquette women's game, pleaded with Blue Demons fans to come out to the game "so that we don't have all of those cheeseheads coming down here again like they did for the men's game."

The DePaul game was the first of three of the next four games on the road. Marquette defeated St. Louis, and then faced Tulane in New Orleans on Jan. 29. That game represented the turning point of the Crean Era, according to Marquette beat reporter Lori Nickel of the *Journal Sentinel*.

"This was the classic game where they could have choked. This is it, they're gonna go down," recalled Nickel. "But they won it [68-66]. Crean was happy after that game. Wade was tweaked a little. They found a way to win. They pulled it out and stayed in the [Conference USA] race.

"This is not status quo, hoping for an NIT," Nickel continued. "That changed a lot. They've turned the corner. They expected to win."

After wins over TCU, St. Louis, and Tulane, the big, bad Cincinnati Bearcats invaded the Bradley Center. No. 4 Cincinnati was Marquette's toughest rival in conference, and the Bearcats were the benchmark for the rest of the conference, having won every regular-season title in the seven-year history of Conference USA. But with Marquette's resurgence, its seven-game winning streak and national ranking, tickets were being snapped up quickly for this game. Many fans were thinking this is the year Marquette would knock off Huggy Bear's Bearcats. The Marquette basketball ticket office in the 1212 Wisconsin Avenue building on campus was busy day and night taking ticket orders. In fact, there was an outside chance that more people would watch this game than any other college basketball game ever played in the state of Wisconsin.

A sellout crowd of 18,698 showed up. Before tip-off, a smiling Crean appeared on the giant Jumbotron screen via videotape, thanking the fans and the students for making the game a sellout, and giving the team a true home-court advantage. It was short, sweet, and sincere. But it was an appreciative video thank-you card from the coach to the fans, and it was put together by Pete McDevitt, then coordinator of basketball operations for the team. Crean began to make the video message a regular part of the pre-game ritual at the Bradley Center.

Inspired by the crowd, Wade and his teammates took control of the game and took it to the Bearcats. When the outcome of the game was determined, George Thompson turned to Steve "The Homer" True and said, "You know who's in the house, Homer?" "Tell me, George, who's in the house?" "Hall of Famer Willie Davis of the Green Bay Packers and another Hall of Famer you might have heard of, Bill Russell," who had addressed the team before the game.

Wade had 25 points, eight rebounds, and three steals to lead MU to a convincing 74-60 win over Cincinnati. After the game, Wade high-fived Russell. Two days later, Wade received more good news: his fiancé Siohvaughn gave birth to their first child—baby boy Zaire. The student section was bathed in gold from the bottom to the top of the Bradley Center. After the win, the students spilled out onto the floor, hoisting Wade onto their shoulders. The happy smile of Wade with the American flag flapping behind him was the big photo in the next day's sports sections. That photo said it all. Marquette had beaten a tough rival soundly on ESPN, a team it needed to beat in order to take that next step up the ladder of respect, especially in conference. The Golden Eagles extended their winning streak to eight games and continued moving up the ranks of the top teams in the country. This Marquette basketball team was earning respect.

The winning streak was then extended to 10 with wins over East Carolina and Southern Mississippi, before Louisville came calling on Saturday, Feb. 16, 2002, with new coach Rick Pitino. And ABC-TV came calling with its number-one announcing team of Dick Vitale and Brent Musburger. It was believed to be the first time that Vitale had ever worked a Marquette game.

Before the game, Crean was asked if he had expected the team to have a 21-3 record in just his third season. "You hope you're gonna get better. You think you're gonna get better. I knew we had a lot of youth. I knew we would be more athletic, and I knew their attitudes were great. But to look at it and say we would be 21-3, I don't think anyone could have picked that," said Crean, he of the combed back, parted hair and new age spectacles. Musburger said, "He looks like Clark Kent." Vitale added: "He's become Superman in this city, baby!"

Once again, the game was the hottest ticket in town. Students and fans began lining up in front the Bradley Center early in the morning for the 2:30 p.m. start. The Louisville game outdrew the Cincinnati game, setting another college basketball attendance record in the state of Wisconsin. A crowd of 18,753, almost all in gold, saw four Marquette players finish in double figures, led by Henry's 23 points. Wade chipped in 11 points, eight rebounds, seven assists, two blocked shots, and two steals. The Golden Eagles' swarming, rotating defense held Louisville's Reece Gaines to 5 points on 1 of 10 shooting.

With 27 seconds remaining in the game, Crean turned around and received a congratulatory handshake from former Michigan State coach Jud Heathcote, who was in the house that day as a guest of his protégé. "The Warriors have done it," exclaimed Musburger. "Eleven in a row. They sweep Louisville 75-63." Marquette extended its home winning streak to 14. After the win, Marquette moved up to No. 9 in the Associated Press Feb. 18 poll, the highest ranking for the program since February of 1979 during the Raymonds Era. Vitale predicted that Marquette would be a Sweet 16 team in the NCAA Tournament.

The nation then had a chance to see Henry and Wade interviewed by Dicky V. Both players talked about taking care of the business at hand, not looking too far ahead to the upcoming game at Cincinnati, and improving every day in practice. Some of it was cliched, or "coach-speak," but both players made their points and expressed themselves well. Both learned their lessons from their coach: Never give an opposing team bulletin board material. As Crean had told ABC's Brad Nessler at the UNC game two years earlier: "We want them on ABC and ESPN and to get to experience this. We want them to get used to being on television."

Marquette then avenged its earlier loss to Charlotte with a 66-52 win in front of 15,371 at the Bradley Center, before heading on the road for two games against Cincinnati and East Carolina. Marquette's 13-game winning streak and Conference USA regular season title were on the line at the Shoemaker Center, where the No. 4 Bearcats lay in wait.

Cincinnati hit Marquette with a 20-4 run to start the game, and pulled away to a 34-24 halftime lead before Marquette made its move in the second half. Marquette led by one with six seconds remaining. Cincinnati called a play during its time out, which left Donald Little open for a shot that he hit with no time left. Marquette's 63-62 heartbreaking loss ended its winning streak and its chance of capturing the Conference USA regular season title. This was a difficult loss to endure, because Marquette played the Bearcats tough in a hostile arena, but once again could not come away with the win. It was a chance for the team to step up that season, but it could not. The loss would stay with the team for the rest of the season.

The hangover from the loss was felt in its last road game at Greenville, North Carolina, where Marquette lost to East Carolina 51-46. While Wade scored 19 points, the team could not rebound from the Cincinnati loss.

When it returned home for Senior Night on Friday, March 1, to play DePaul, Marquette broke the attendance record that was set at the Louisville game when a solid gold crowd of 18,788 saw the Golden Eagles dominate the Blue Demons 72-53. Seniors Henry, Nnamaka, Harris, and Diggs were given a big thank-you by the fans for their contributions in helping return the program to prominence. Marquette held DePaul to just 29.6 percent shooting in the win. It was also the last game that Pat Kennedy would coach at DePaul. The following week he announced his resignation.

The third straight sellout concluded an undefeated home season, 16-0 (one win was at US Cellular Arena). It swelled attendance for all home games to 191,650—an average of 12,777 per game. Marquette's season record was 26-6, the best since McGuire's 1975–76 team finished 26-2. One of Crean's goals was met: protecting home-court advantage.

The team made another big improvement: it finished the season with a 5-5 road record, and was gaining confidence that it could win on the road.

Marquette could now prepare for the Conference USA Tournament in Cincinnati. Once again, the Golden Eagles had a chance to win the conference tournament and avenge losing the regular season title to Cincinnati, after having it seemingly in hand. Marquette finished the conference schedule at 13-3, which was the most wins by a Marquette team in league play and earned the Golden Eagles a No. 2 seed in the C-USA Tournament.

In its March 7 first round match, Marquette faced Louisville and won for the third time, 84-76. Henry torched Louisville for 24 points on 50 percent shooting. Wade added 11 points, nine rebounds, three assists, a steal, and a blocked shot. Diener added 11 and Nnamaka 10. Henry continued his assault the next day in an 85-73 win over Houston, scoring 27 points on 9 of 16 shooting, and added six assists. Wade had 18 and Nnamaka 14. In addition to his 55 points, Henry had also averaged a lengthy 38 minutes of playing time for the two games.

No. 10 Marquette then faced No. 5 Cincinnati for the third time that season at a packed, pro-Cincinnati Firstar Center. There were smatterings of gold in the arena, but it was clearly a very partisan Bearcat crowd. Crean said before the game that Marquette had to be able to withstand Cincinnati's runs in order to have a chance to win.

It was a tough game, with the trash-talking and woofing going back and forth between Bearcat All-America Steve Logan and Henry and Wade and Leonard Stokes. Cincinnati rode its 5 of 7 shooting from three-point range to take a 31-24 halftime lead. Wade drew oohs and ahhs with his myriad moves and dunks for six points, three rebounds, and an assist. Henry's 0 for 4 performance in the half had CBS analyst Dan Bonner asking his play-by-play partner Gus Johnson, "Is Henry tired?" His shots, including the patented little runners in the paint, were not falling as they had in the previous two games.

During the regular season, teams that had played zone defense against Marquette were, more often than not, successful. After the Bearcats switched from their traditional man-to-man defense to a zone, it slowed down the Golden Eagles, thus not allowing Wade to take over the game in transition as he had in the first half. There were several hard fouls on both sides, and the game deteriorated to the point where Cincinnati freshman Jason Maxiell hit Henry in the midsection with a punch toward the end of the game, sending him reeling to the floor. "This is no lovefest here," said Johnson, who added, "He [Maxiell] will be a marked man next year." Merritt and Wade (16 points) both fouled out. Marquette showed it would not be cowed by Cincinnati and gave as well as it got, but the team still could not get over that hump of beating Cincinnati on the road. The Bearcats pulled away for a 77-63 win and the Conference USA Tournament Championship.

"I have a feeling Marquette will remember this game and mark down Cincinnati on the calendar for next season," predicted Johnson.

The Road to the Final Four is not a smooth one. It is a rocky road filled with detours, pitfalls, and potholes. And expectations. Basketball teams struggle with injuries, unhappy players who transfer, losing streaks, and just plain bad luck as they navigate their way to that final Monday night of the season when they hope to be the last team standing as CBS caps its telecast with "One Shining Moment," the official anthem of the NCAA Tournament.

After the tough C-USA Tournament loss, Marquette regrouped on Selection Sunday for the NCAA pairings. While many Marquette fans felt that the team deserved at least a No. 4 seed (if not a 3), most everyone agreed that the team was going to get a decent seed and stay close to home. The thinking was that getting to the championship game of the Conference USA tourney would seal a high bid. What hurt Marquette, though, was its strength of schedule, or lack thereof, during the season. However, the team's RPI was a solid 22.

The team gathered at a private room at TGIFriday's in Milwaukee's Miller Park to watch the pairings. Marquette received a No. 5 seed for the NCAA Tournament, and would be playing its first game against the University of Tulsa in St. Louis. As per the new "Pod" system that the NCAA debuted that tournament, higher-seeded teams would be kept closer to their schools' locations in the sub-regional rounds. Marquette was seeded in the East Regional, even though the team was playing its first-round game in St. Louis.

For Tom Crean and his hard-working basketball team, this next step on the journey to respectability would begin March 14, 2002, at the Edward Jones Dome in St. Louis. It was the team's first NCAA Tournament appearance since 1997, and the team's reward for a successful 26-6 campaign. There was reason to celebrate.

There was also a kind of cockeyed optimism for this Marquette team. Many fans who logged on to the DoddsOnSports.com web site, which is affiliated with Rivals.com, felt the team could reach the Sweet 16, even though none of the Golden Eagles had ever played in an NCAA Tournament game. The fact that this was the 25th anniversary of Marquette's national championship and the Final Four was being played in Atlanta, had Warrior Nation dreaming of ANOTHER rainy night in Georgia. Expectations were obviously very high heading into this tournament.

Marquette was a 4-point favorite against a very athletic—and experienced—University of Tulsa team that rebounded well and had good three-point shooters. The Golden Hurricanes represented the Western Athletic Conference (WAC) and were coached by John Phillips, who had just completed his first season as a head coach at age 54.

"The day before at the shoot-around, the team looked so confident and ready and prepared," recalled Nickel. "I thought that I would be going to the Sweet 16 that tournament."

Unfortunately, Marquette's first-round game showcased some of its weaknesses, especially against a team as quick and athletic on the boards as Tulsa. And experienced. The Golden Hurricanes had played in the previous three NCAA Tournaments, and only Duke and Cincinnati had won more games than Tulsa in the previous three seasons.

Tulsa took a 34-30 lead into halftime. The Golden Hurricanes were consistently beating Marquette to the boards for crucial second-chance points. Tulsa's confidence was evident in its transition game, where it was running and gunning. Marquette was close to being run off the floor when it started to make a comeback at the three-quarter mark of the game.

Both teams traded baskets until Tulsa scored on a drive down the lane by Greg Harrington as Nnamaka was bumping him to try to disrupt his shot. The basket put Tulsa ahead by two, 71-69, with 11 seconds remaining in regulation. Before Tulsa scored, Crean had called a play during a Marquette time-out, so that the Golden Hurricanes would not be able to set up their defense when Marquette came down the floor.

Marquette had three guards on the floor in Henry, Wade, and Diener. Henry brought the ball into the front court where he looked at Crean, who signaled to the guard by repeatedly touching his hand to his elbow and nodding confidently toward him, as if to say, "You know what to do."

"Cordell seemed like he had forgotten the play or wasn't sure what it was," recalled Marquette radio play-by-play announcer Steve "The Homer" True.

Tulsa did a good job of keeping Marquette's three-point marksmen farther away from the three-point line than they wanted to be.

Henry moved to the top of the three-point arc, quickly looked over Tulsa's defense and dribbled toward Wade, who had scored 18 points and pulled down seven rebounds during the game. "He [Henry] got the ball into Dwyane Wade's hands and assumed he would attack," remembered True.

Wade took the ball and began dribbling toward the left baseline, stopped, and gave the ball back to Henry, who dribbled back toward the arc and quickly passed to Diener at the top of the arc with just over 3.5 seconds left. "Diener had it, but the defense had it covered," said True.

Diener then launched a desperation NBA-three-pointer as Wade quickly ran underneath the basket. The shot fell short as Wade tried to either complete an alley-oop jam or grab the rebound. The ball hit Harris on the head and bounced out of bounds as he tried to grab it. Wade hung on the rim so long, it was as if he did not want to let it go and have the season end. The indecisiveness of Henry, Wade, and Diener in those final seconds made the basketball look like a hot potato. It seemed that nobody wanted the ball when the game was on the line.

Tulsa advanced in one of the tournament's No. 12 over No. 5 seed upsets that day to face Kentucky. Marquette went home much sooner than everyone expected. "It was a disappointing finish," lamented True.

"They showed inexperience in playing in the postseason," noted Nickel. "I remember walking into the locker room and those players looked like they had died. They just looked like they had all been run over by a semi.

"Shock. Disappointment. They looked like they had messed up their biggest opportunity. They had a really good season. Did they think they were going to win the national title? I didn't remember ever seeing such devastation. You usually don't see that devastated a reaction after a first-round loss."

And it would not be unusual for a coach to duck fans after such a tough loss, but neither Crean nor his staff did.

"An hour and a half after the game," recalled Larry Six, "we headed back to the Edward Jones Dome for the next session of games. My son, Mark, started to cross the street and we saw Coach Crean and the coaches walking back to the hotel. Coach Crean saw Mark, who was wearing his Marquette T-shirt. He walked back and thanked Mark for his support. He then saw me, came over and thanked me for coming down to support the team. A lot of coaches would not have taken the time. We really have a guy who not only cares about the team, but the people and fans who support the team."

Like the North Carolina loss at Chapel Hill a year earlier, this was another game Marquette had to go through in order to learn what it takes to win at the next level. It was an important experience that would mold the team for the next season, as difficult as it was for the team to accept. Experience is a difficult teacher, and these players had never had this experience before. They did not know what it took to advance in a one-and-done situation. It was another measuring-stick game that taught the team what it needed to do to reach the next level. It was a season where for every two steps forward, the team took one step back.

Marquette had earned the respect of Tulsa and the rest of the nation in that exciting, memorable season. It finished No. 12 in the AP and No. 18 in the ESPN/USA Today polls. In fact, Marquette was in AP's top 25 for 12 weeks during the season. It was the first time since 1995–96 that the team finished the season in the top 25, and the highest ranking since 1978–79, when the team finished the season at No. 10. ∎

CHAPTER THREE:
GOIN' UPTOWN

Goin' Uptown was Al McGuire's phrase for moving up in the world, whether it was improving one's station in life, heading to the NCAA Tournament, or moving up to the elite of college basketball. After the successful 26-7 campaign, Marquette Nation felt that the team was Goin' Uptown.

There also had been talk that Wade might try for the NBA draft after finishing his first full season as a collegian. The consensus was that his perimeter game needed some work. Also, at his size (he was listed at 6'5") Wade was considered a "tweener"—between a guard and a small forward. He also played out of control at times during the season, which resulted in turnovers. Other than that, the only thing anyone could complain about was that Wade was too unselfish. He needed to take more shots, it was said. For his first full year of college competition, though, Wade played outstanding basketball. He led his team in scoring (17.8 ppg), rebounding (6.6 rpg), assists (3.4 apg), steals (2.46 spg—first in Conference USA), and blocked shots (1.1 bpg). He scored in double figures in 31 of his 32 games and had nine games of 20 points or more.

Marquette students and fans anxiously awaited Wade's decision on whether he would declare for the draft. He held a spring press conference on campus to make his announcement. Prior to that season, few people outside of Marquette and a few NBA scouts who attended the team practices at the Old Gym, knew how good of a player Wade really was. So, before the Great Alaska Shootout, Wade had pretty much flown under the national radar.

Wade took the first round loss to Tulsa personally, and announced that he would return for his junior season at Marquette. He made a lot of people happy, including Crean and his staff, which had given Wade all of the information he and his family needed to make his decision. Wade was not only determined to improve the various aspects of his game, but to make sure there would be no repeat performance of what happened in the NCAA Tournament. Wade was not about to let it happen again, if he could help it.

But there were enough awards to go around for Wade and the team to assuage their hurt feelings after the season. Wade received Honorable Mention All-America from the Associated Press as well as Newcomer of the Year from *Basketball Times*. Crean won the Ray Meyer Award as Conference USA Coach of the Year; NABC District 11 Coach of the Year; UWBWA District 5 Coach of the Year; and was a finalist for *ESPN Magazine*'s College Coach of the Year.

Crean's efforts to create a home-court advantage were working beautifully. During the season, waves of gold T-shirts cascaded up the student section in the Bradley Center from the lower bowl all the way to the upper reaches of the stadium. Marquette and its very loyal fan base and burgeoning student attendance, helped bring sellouts to the Bradley Center for the first time ever during the 2001–02 season.

The good news of Wade's return, however, was offset by the departure of three of his teammates. Menard, Howard, and childhood friend Odartey Blankson all decided to transfer. The three were reportedly not happy with their lack of playing time and wanted to be more involved in the offense. Add to that the four graduating seniors, and Marquette was losing seven players from a team that had advanced to the NCAA Tournament for the first time in five years. There would be only 10 roster players on scholarship, leaving Crean shorthanded for the upcoming season, which would make it more difficult in the coming season with a tougher schedule.

The news of the transfers surprised many, and there were questions about Crean's relationships with his players and how he was treating them. There were concerns that Blankson's departure for UNLV, especially after a productive sophomore season at small forward, would hurt Marquette's inside game, which was exacerbated by the losses of Nnamaka and Harris to graduation. What was even more surprising is that Blankson had just been named one of the team's captains for the 2002–03 season. In fact, Crean told Dan Bonner and Gus Johnson, of CBS, before the Conference USA Tournament Championship, that Blankson was "the heart and soul of this team and the toughest player on the floor."

"Odartey Blankson left because he wanted to shoot more and wanted the ball more. It [Crean's system] was more than Odartey could handle," explained True.

Wade may have been losing his longtime teammate and friend at Humphrey Hall, but he was getting a new roommate in his bride, Siohvaughn, with whom he would move into an off-campus apartment with their young son, Zaire.

Wade also had arthroscopic surgery to repair a slight tear of the meniscus in his left knee, which had bothered him all year long. Merritt had surgery on his shoulder.

Not knowing how Crean's talented, incoming Top-40 class of Steve Novak (Brown Deer, Wisconsin), Chris Grimm (Brighton, Michigan), Karon Bradley (Katy, Texas) and Joe Chapman (Sauk Village, Illinois) would help the team, Crean still had returning junior forward Merritt and Mississippi State transfer Robert Jackson, who would be eligible to play after having sat out the previous year when he returned to Milwaukee. Jackson's 6'10", 265-pound "Aircraft Carrier" presence allowed Merritt to return to his natural power forward position.

"We got in on Karon at a late time but we were lucky enough to have him see the opportunity that he had here," said Crean of Bradley, a 5'11" combination guard, who averaged 28 points a game his senior year at Cypress Springs High School. "If he can emerge the way we hope he can, he gives us an opportunity not only to play with Travis at the one spot, but also the chance to go small and play three guards which I thought was successful for us last year."

Chapman, a tough 6'4" guard, is effective at both ends of the floor. The Bloom (Illinois) High School graduate took three straight charges in an all-star game where Crean was recruiting. Crean said, "That's the kind of guy I want playing on my team."

"Joe is a tough-minded, physically-imposing guard who wants nothing but to get better. He went from being a power forward in his early years in high school to a pretty good shooting guard as time went on," Crean noted.

Chris Grimm, a 6'10" player from Brighton (Michigan) High School was the fourth leading shot-blocker in Michigan high school history. "That is something that has not been a strength of ours the past few years. After having shoulder surgery this off-season, his progress was set back, but I feel that he will be able to help us in a lot of ways," Crean predicted.

Another question mark in the minds of Marquette Nation was whether sophomore shooting guard Diener could fill the void at the point left by Henry. During Crean's first two years, Henry had become an unapologetic leader on the floor. He could pass as well as shoot the three-pointer. A fearless competitor, it was generally agreed that Henry would be missed. Could Diener—the shooting point guard—fill the role of point guard, shooter, and floor general? A tough trifecta.

While Diener was a terrific shooter, it was argued by the posters on DoddsonSports.com that he had too slight of a build and was not the penetrator Henry was. Could Diener handle the point? Diener, though, had something else to play for: his half brother, Dan, who had died a year earlier. To honor his memory, Diener was changing his uniform number from 10 to 34—the number Dan wore when he played. To continue to honor McGuire's memory, the team changed its AL patches to white and had them stitched to the top center of their jerseys.

As fans mulled over the point guard conundrum, another question that was resolved was Crean's contract extension. The extension and Crean's salary were not released because Marquette is a private institution, but reportedly another five years would be tacked on to the remaining year of his original contract. Suffice it to say, everyone was happy. While Crean was signing his own contract extension, he lost another assistant. This time it was Tod Kowalczyk, who was hired to coach UW–Green Bay. As tough as it was for Crean to have another close assistant leave, it said much about the quality of the assistants he recruited, and how he had prepared them to be ready when a school called looking for a good head coach.

"It is very rewarding for me, but it also says a lot about the young people in this program. They have played well enough and worked hard enough to give athletic directors and college presidents at other universities the belief in hiring people like Tim Buckley and Tod Kowalczyk. As a coaching staff, we do our best to prepare these young men for all facets of the game and all facets of life. The university gives us the opportunity to work on our craft and for myself as a head coach, it is important that I give all our coaches the opportunity to gain the knowledge and insight and have the responsibilities that they need to run their own program."

Crean's commitment to promote and help raise money for the McGuire Center continued unabated. The new practice facility would replace the Old Gym, which was really an antiquated ROTC building. He was part of the committee for "Al's Big Dance," a gala, star-studded fundraising event at the Bradley Center on April 18, 2002, that featured such notables as Billy Packer, Dick Enberg, Rick Majerus, U.S. Sen. Herb Kohl (who owns the Milwaukee Bucks), and friends of the Marquette and McGuire families. The $350-a-plate event raised $700,000 and moved fundraising for the center to another level. The success of the event set the stage for a groundbreaking on the site (Wells Street, between 12th and 13th streets) in May of 2002 by Al's widow, Pat, his daughter, Noreen, and other family members. Interested fans could watch the progress of the center each day on a McGuirecam that could be accessed through the university's web site (gomarquette.edu). The foundation for the McGuire Center was laid later that summer.

With all of the responsibilities Crean had undertaken, he still found a way to stay on top of details that most coaches would probably delegate to underlings. While he was in Cleveland in June, Crean placed a phone call to wish longtime Marquette season-ticket holder Dr. John Brennan a happy 80th birthday, much to the good doctor's surprise. "He has that personal touch," commented Dr. Brennan. Crean has made a habit of writing down the names, dates, and places where he meets people during his day so that he does not forget them.

Even with all of the questions surrounding the team, there was still a buzz of anticipation about the 2002–03 basketball season, the 85th in Marquette history. In addition to Crean's recruiting class being touted among the top 40 in the country, Wade was being named to the first team of almost every All-America preseason squad. He was also being listed as a preseason finalist for the Wooden, Naismith, and Oscar Robertson awards.

Diener and Terry Sanders played during the summer months with the People-to-People All-Stars that toured Australia. "We had Travis go overseas because we wanted to put the ball back in his hands as a point guard and get him the feeling of running a team," explained Crean. "I think it is going to be crucial for him to emerge in that 'I run the show' point guard mentality that makes everyone around him better.

"His leadership, both on and off the floor, will be very important. That is a lot to expect of someone who has played just one year of college basketball, but we feel that he has that potential.

"Frequently in sports, the previous year's success leads to the upcoming year's expectations," continued Crean. "Although we have some experience returning, we will have a very young team as judged by the fact that of the 10 scholarship players we have, seven have played one year or less of college basketball. Our lone senior, Robert Jackson, has not played a game for us this year."

Utah Coach Rick Majerus weighed in with his own take on Crean's young team. Due to a prior commitment, Majerus could not make the annual Cyganiak Summer Golf Outing. In his faxed letter, Majerus had high praise for Wade, Diener, Jackson, and Novak, and predicted big things for the Golden Eagles.

"I'm really pulling for the team this year. Tom has an outstanding club and quite frankly, it could very well make the Final Four. Dwyane is even better than Doc Rivers. I tried to recruit the little point guard from Fond du Lac. That kid is a real keeper and sensational. The forward from Brown Deer that is coming on board reminds me of Keith Van Horn. You're going to really enjoy this year's squad, but the real secret, and trust me when I tell you that he could be a first-round pick without question, is the boy they have who transferred from Mississippi by way of Washington High School.

"Maybe if Al was smiling upon us in the sky, the Utes could make the tournament, too, this year. I'm going to be in New Orleans and I expect to see you there wearing blue and gold. This is Marquette's year if there ever was one, and it is because of the loyal alumni like you, who revel so much in their success, both in the academic arena as well as on the court."

The anticipation of the coming season was responsible for a big surge in season-ticket sales among students. The Marquette Fanatic Student

Packages set a record with 3,128 sold. Some 5,000 students and fans attended the fourth annual Midnight Madness with special guests Jay Bilas and Boston Celtics Hall of Famer Bill Russell. The players donned blue, white, and gold wigs and attempted to entertain the fans with their own brand of karaoke. It looked like a bad imitation of Parliament/Funkadelic, and the U.S. Cellular Arena was the Mothership that night.

After several years off the national radar, Marquette, with only 10 scholarship players, was being mentioned once again in various top 25 preseason polls, including *Street & Smith*, AP (No. 18), *ESPN* (No. 19), *Athlon*, *Basketball News*, and *Sports Illustrated*. MU was ranked as high as 13th in the country, a recognition and respect that had long eluded the program. In the *Chicago Tribune*'s College Basketball Season Preview, a large color photo featured Wade in full flight below the headline, "Soaring Eagle." Skip Myslenski noted in his accompanying story that Wade was "The best that Chicagoland basketball had to offer." He was now getting national recognition for himself and the Golden Eagles.

Marquette also was slated for at least nine televised games, including national and regional broadcasts on ABC, ESPN, and ESPN2. That was another building block for the program: national recognition.

"Television is the determining factor as to whether a program is headed in an upward direction," explained Crean. "There is no doubt that the television coverage that we are receiving now on the national, regional, and local levels will give us the feeling that we are building something of prominence.

"We also know that you have to be competitive and have the opportunity to win in order for television to come knocking. Fortunately, that has happened and we look forward to the opportunity to show the nation what Marquette basketball is all about as we continue to improve this year."

The only lingering negative for the team was that Schwab's condition had worsened, despite all of the medications and work he was putting into his treatment regimen. Doctors informed him in September that a lung transplant was his only option to survive. He was then put on two lung transplant waiting lists. In addition to the wait, Schwab's potential donor would have to be the same age, blood type, and body size as he. While he waited, Schwab had to stick to a strict daily 10-hour schedule, and have a small, portable oxygen tank with hoses leading into his nose. He also used inhalers to deal with the half-hour-plus coughing fits that are symptoms of IPF.

Before the team's exhibition games, Crean had asked Schwab to locate a photograph of the Louisiana Superdome. Schwab surfed internet sites until he found one that was selling such photos. He ordered the photo, had it blown up, and gave it to Crean.

After Marquette's win over the Wisconsin All-Stars in its second exhibition game, Crean showed the players the photo in the locker room. He asked all of those who believed they could get to the Superdome that season to win the Final Four to sign the photo, and those who did not think they could get there to not sign it. "All of the players signed it," according to Todd Rosiak, Marquette's beat reporter for the *Journal Sentinel*. The photo went on road trips with the players and was placed in a prominent place in the locker room before games. But the players and coaches kept the goal to themselves.

According to beat reporter Lori Nickel, the goal was not something the players shared with the media. The team and season goals were released on a "need to know" basis.

While such a motivational ploy was looked on as gimmicky or corny, Crean sincerely believed that the visualization of a goal is one of the most important aspects in trying to accomplish it. After all, he minored in psychology at Central Michigan University. The big difference between McGuire and Crean, in their approaches to motivation, was that Crean appealed to his players' minds while McGuire appealed to his players' baser instincts, including manhood, pride, and fear, according to longtime McGuire assistant Hank Raymonds. McGuire did not use physical props to get his points across.

The previous season, Marquette was fortunate in that it suffered no serious injuries. There were some nagging injuries, but for the most part the players played through them. Wade and Merritt had recuperated nicely from their respective surgeries during the off-season. But after the second exhibition game, freshman Karon Bradley would have his left knee scoped.

Not having Bradley would put additional pressure on Diener, but the team was ready to open the regular season. The Golden Eagles were slated to play Villanova in the "Coaches versus Cancer Classic" at Madison Square

Garden, Friday evening, Nov. 15. This was going to be Wade's coming out party at basketball's Mecca—The Gahden. The last time Marquette's name was on the Madison Square Garden marquee was for the 1995 NIT Championship game against Virginia Tech.

And Wade did not disappoint.

Wade wowed the Garden's basketball sophisticates and an ESPN2 audience with his play on both ends of the floor, as No. 18 Marquette defeated Villanova 73-61. The Wildcats, though, were playing without star Gary Buchanon. Wade's 17 points, five rebounds, four assists, two steals, and no turnovers were good enough for him to be named the game's Most Valuable Player. Marquette let a 20-point lead slip away to nine with three minutes left. Marquette was also outrebounded 53-43, and 31 of those 53 were offensive rebounds. But Marquette displayed a poise it would exhibit all year and won the game. The way Marquette won set the stage for future games. The Golden Eagles did not get rattled down the stretch.

It was said that Wade's maturity on the floor was a result of his now being a husband and a father. It was noted that he did not play as much out of control. While his turnover totals still led the team, they were not as numerous as in his first full season when he also led the team in scoring, rebounding, assists, steals, and blocked shots.

"The areas of improvement that he needed to focus upon during the off-season were perimeter shooting, tightening up his ball handling, becoming a better on-ball defender, and realizing how good a rebounder he can really be," said Crean of his All-America. "That may sound funny to say about a guy who led your team in rebounding, but Dwyane could be tremendous in that area."

Marquette's win over Villanova was a nice opening act for Marquette's journey to the elite of college basketball during the 2002–03 season. It was another test the team passed on its way to learning how to play in the spotlight. The team moved up to No. 16 in the next AP poll and No. 19 in the ESPN/USA TODAY poll. While the poll numbers were nice and flattering, Crean wanted the team to continue to bring the same intensity to its upcoming practices and games as it did for Villanova. Crean, not wanting to take anything for granted, was looking for a consistency of effort for each and every opponent, not just for the big boys.

The previous season, Marquette had been criticized for its less than difficult schedule, which, to be fair, included its share of Woffords, Coppin States, and Appalachian States of the college basketball world. For 2002–03 Crean scheduled not only Villanova, but a return date with Wake Forest at the Bradley Center and a home-and-home with Notre Dame to revive that legendary rivalry. Marquette has played Notre Dame in basketball more than any other school in Fighting Irish history, and alums at both schools had continually asked Crean and his Irish counterpart Mike Brey when the rivalry would be resumed. The teams had not played since 1997. Defending Big Ten champion Wisconsin was scheduled at the Bradley Center, in addition to Marquette's Conference USA slate, featuring Cincinnati, Louisville, and improving St. Louis and DePaul, the latter under new coach Dave Leitao.

Marquette went on to win its fourth straight Blue & Gold Classic, by defeating Coppin State and Texas–San Antonio. Wade had 24 points, seven rebounds, and four steals to lead all scorers against Coppin. In the Championship game against Texas–San Antonio, he scored 32 points, had 13 rebounds, seven assists, a steal, and blocked a shot.

Those passing by the construction site at the McGuire Center could see progress there, too. One wall was up, then another. It was a steady process that paralleled that of the basketball team.

The Golden Eagles then welcomed Henry Domercant and the Eastern Illinois University Panthers. The expected showdown between Wade and Domercant, who led the country in scoring the year before with 26.4 points per game, was all the talk. While Domercant scored 27, Wade had 28, with five rebounds, six assists, and three steals. Marquette easily defeated the Panthers 97-74, which served as a tuneup for the much anticipated game at South Bend against Notre Dame, another 2002 NCAA Tournament team.

Against a quicker Notre Dame team, Marquette looked flat-footed. All night long, the Golden Eagles had no answer for point guard Chris Thomas, the quicksilver sophomore who could penetrate, pass, and shoot the three. He lit up Marquette for 32 points on 12 of 18 shooting (including 5 of 8 from three-point land), and added 10 assists. Notre Dame, it seemed, hit just about everything that it put up, shooting 50 percent from the floor, and headed to the locker room with a 42-30 halftime lead. Marquette staged a comeback in the second half, narrowing the lead to four points, but Notre Dame then put the game away. Marquette had four players in double figures, led by Wade's 19 points, Diener's 18, and Jackson and Merritt with 12 apiece. That would be the last time a team would shoot 50 percent or better against Marquette during the regular season.

It was Marquette's worst regular-season loss since the North Carolina game the year before, but the difference this time was that Marquette was within striking distance before Notre Dame put the game away. The loss was disappointing, but Marquette ran into a hot team that night. Marquette was ranked, and the Fighting Irish were in the midst of defeating three ranked teams within a period of 10 days: Marquette, Texas, and defending national champion Maryland.

Bo Ryan and his unranked 6-1 Badgers then paid a visit to the Bradley Center Dec. 14 to face the 5-1, No. 16 Golden Eagles. Marquette celebrated the 50th anniversary of Marquette's first national championship, the 1952 National Catholic Collegiate Champions, who were coached by Tex Winter. Back in '52, the 28-year-old Winter was the youngest college basketball coach in America. Now an octogenarian, who was Phil Jackson's assistant with the Chicago Bulls and L.A. Lakers, Winter returned for the celebration along with 18 of the original 20 team members, who were known as the Hilltoppers. That game was just the first night where Marquette would welcome back the champions of its basketball past to help inspire Crean's young squad. It was another sellout, with 18,677 in attendance, and much of the Badgers' red wave relegated to the upper reaches of the Bradley Center.

So inspired, Marquette came out and played an intense defensive game against Wisconsin. It was close throughout. Marquette had a three-point lead late in the game, when Crean called an isolation play for Wade. The junior attacked the basket, was fouled and made both free throws, giving the Golden Eagles a 59-54 lead. That was the key play of the game as Marquette went on to win by nine, 63-54. Marquette held Wisconsin to 36.5 percent shooting, while the Golden Eagles shot 52.2 percent. Wade scored 25 and Kirk Penney was held to seven, after having burned Marquette for 33 a year earlier in Madison.

Crean and the team took another step with the win, avenging a loss at Madison the year before. It was the first time Crean had defeated the Badgers, who would go on to win the Big Ten regular season title. Wisconsin had beaten Marquette four straight. But not this night. It was also Marquette's 20th straight win at the Bradley Center.

In order to accommodate its growing list of television games, Marquette switched its originally scheduled away date with East Carolina to late December, which made it the team's first conference game of the season, much earlier than the Golden Eagles wanted. It also would begin the toughest road stretch for the Golden Eagles, in which they would play five out of six games on the road between Dec. 30, 2002, and Jan. 18, 2003.

Even though Marquette had four players in double figures, led by Wade's 21 points, and a solid performance from Todd Townsend (11 points, six rebounds, and five assists), Marquette shockingly lost at East Carolina for the second straight year. Wade helped lead Marquette in a furious, come-from-behind effort, but his three-point attempt that would have sent the game into overtime fell short. The win sent Pirates' fans into a frenzy at the packed Minges Coliseum in Greenville. The loss caused a deluge of suicide-like posts on the DoddsonSports.com web site from Marquette fans. Once again, Marquette came up empty in the Tar Heel State.

The shock was that a ranked (No. 12 ESPN/USA TODAY; No. 13 AP) and talented team let down the way Marquette did. What added injury to insult was that it was a conference loss. Marquette fans were fearing that the loss would put the team behind the eight ball in an expected tight Conference USA race with both Cincinnati and Louisville, where each win and each loss is crucial. And on top of that, it was the team's second road loss.

Marquette then went out and lost its third straight road game at Dayton, in overtime. Wade started out poorly, but once again helped lead a nice second-half comeback. Robert Jackson took over the scoring reins from Wade with a 19-point performance, including his 1,000th career point. Wade had a double-double with 17 points and 10 rebounds, Scott Merritt had 16, Townsend 11, and Diener 10. Wade was in the habit of letting the game come to him. He did not appear on the surface to be concerned or show emotion if he had played a subpar first half. He somehow seemed to bring everything together in the second half. There was further concern because Jackson hurt his tailbone when he fell during the game.

After the three straight road losses, Crean decided the team needed some inspirational motivation. So, he showed them the Tom Hanks film "Saving Private Ryan" during one of the practices before the team headed to St. Louis for its next road game.

Questions were being raised in the local media and fan web sites about Marquette's road woes. Some were predicting that the sky was falling. Why can't Marquette win on the road? But Marquette had a reputation for bouncing back after tough losses.

The turning point of the season was about to take place in St. Louis. The Golden Eagles traveled to the Savvis Center to face the Billikens. A fourth road loss would have been devastating to the team's chances to win the conference. Before the game, Crean took a black baseball bat out of his bag of motivational tricks, one that he had purchased at Miller Park during the baseball season, and presented it to the team. The words, CHARACTER, UNSELFISHNESS, and TOUGHNESS were inscribed on the bat, which was Crean's answer to the magical "Wonderboy" bat Robert Redford used in *The Natural*. Crean asked all of his players to sign the bat, and it was brought with the team on road trips along with the photo of the Louisiana Superdome. Crean was hoping that he picked out a winner.

The team, already shorthanded at point guard, was still awaiting the return of a healthy Karon Bradley. The freshman had gradually worked his way into decent playing minutes before his arthroscopic surgery. His recovery was slower than anticipated. When Bradley did return, it was for short stints where he would show flashes of the brilliance that caught Coach Crean's attention when he was recruiting him. But then he needed fluid drained from the knee.

As a result, Diener was logging heavy minutes at the point, spelled occasionally by Wade and freshman Joe Chapman. Diener's shot was not falling, leading to speculation that his minutes were taking a toll on his offensive production, especially from three-point range. As longtime WISN radio analyst George Thompson confidently predicted after Diener had bricked a few shots during a home game, "Those shots will start to fall as the season progresses."

During the first half, Wade, as was the case in previous games against the Billikens, was being closely guarded. During one sequence, he and another player slammed into each other and Wade fell to the floor, writhing in pain. He injured his ribs and had to leave the game.

As Wade was slowly helped off the floor, Diener—who was playing against his cousin, Drew—huddled up his teammates and told them they were going to win the game. The fresh-faced college sophomore, who still looked like a high school sophomore, showed the leadership and savvy of a senior. Merritt had a double-double (14 points, 11 rebounds), Jackson had 13 points, Diener 10, and maybe the biggest contribution of all came from freshman Steve Novak, who stepped up with 10 points, including four clutch free throws at the end of the game to seal the team's first road win of the conference season. Wade once again was held under double figures by a tough Billikens' squad, scoring just six points. But the team showed that it could win without Wade. He did not have to carry the load as he did during his first year. Marquette was getting balanced scoring and nice contributions from the talented freshmen off the bench. Travis won the family match this night, as cousin Drew did not get a basket, rebound, assist, or steal.

On Jan. 11, Marquette returned to the Bradley Center for the first time since Dec. 28 for George Thompson Appreciation Night. Many of the 16,395 fans received a replica of his No. 24 jersey as a memento, and Thompson received his own keepsake: an oil painting of the St. Joan of Arc Chapel.

The University of South Florida was the sacrificial lamb that night, as Marquette won easily 96-63. Marquette took a 43-20 halftime lead and continued to build on it the rest of the night. Wade's 21 points led another balanced attack as five Golden Eagles scored in double figures. Diener had 13 points, 12 assists, and just one turnover in 31 minutes. That night saw another familiar face rejoin the team on the bench: Jon Harris. Crean once again showed his loyalty to a former player by inviting him to join the team as a graduate assistant after Harris had finished his overseas playing career.

The Golden Eagles then headed to New Orleans to face Tulane in tiny Fogelman Arena. After the team practice, Crean had the bus driver take a detour. Instead of taking the team back to the hotel, he had the driver go to the Louisiana Superdome, site of the 2003 Final Four. The players had taken the picture of the Superdome with them everywhere they went during the season, and now they could see the arena for themselves. Utilizing his powers of visualization, Crean wanted the players to see the Superdome up close and get used to seeing it. The players were taken on a tour of the spaceship-shaped building and shown where the court and their team bench would be the night of the Final Four. Inspired by the detour, Wade then went out and tied his career high in points that night when he scored 35. Wade added five rebounds, an assist, two blocks, and two steals in Marquette's 85-73 win. Wade exploded, and the team was starting to think big. If seeing is believing, Crean wanted his players to believe.

Marquette overcame another big obstacle on Saturday evening, Jan. 18, when it took on the UNC–Charlotte 49ers in Halton Arena, in front of 19,607 49er fanatics. Wade and Jackson led Marquette with 20 and 13 points, respectively. Freshmen Novak and Chapman came off the bench to add six points and a big three-pointer, respectively. Marquette won the game 67-64.

But the last 10 seconds were a little too close for comfort for the Golden Eagles. With Marquette ahead 67-64, and just over two seconds remaining, Novak was at the line for two free throws. Novak missed, and the 49ers pulled down the rebound and quickly called time-out. Then, with just 1.7 seconds left, Wade stole the inbounds pass to end the game.

It was the first win ever by a Marquette team against a Carolina team in the Tar Heel State. The Tar Heel monkey was now off Marquette's back. The win evened the team's road record at 3-3 for the season, and gave the Golden Eagles great confidence going home to the Bradley Center.

And if anyone doubted Steve Novak's work ethic, it certainly was in evidence after everyone left Halton Arena. He came out of the locker room and kept shooting free throws by himself in the empty arena until he was satisfied.

One of Marquette's more impressive defensive displays took place on Saturday afternoon, Jan. 25, against DePaul, during "Al's Day." The game was played almost two years to the day after McGuire's death. Some 17,025 (nearly all who attended received commemorative gold caps) saw Marquette dominate the Blue Demons, 82-51, though the Golden Eagles lost the battle of the boards (they were outrebounded 28-19). Todd Townsend set the tone early with four three-pointers in the first half. Marquette (No. 20 AP; No. 19 ESPN/USA TODAY) dove for loose balls and mixed up its defenses, forcing the Blue Demons into double-digit turnovers and poor shooting. While Marquette had a 32-18 halftime lead, DePaul had more turnovers (11) than field goals (six).

Wade scored 21 points and had seven steals, five coming in the first half. With just over a minute remaining in the game, DePaul's frustration was such that Milwaukee native Quemont Greer fouled Wade as he was going in for a exclamation-mark dunk. Greer grabbed Wade's shoulder and pulled him to the floor. Greer was hit with an intentional foul, which also was his fifth. Wade's performance that afternoon impressed ESPN Plus analyst Stephen Bardo. "Dwyane Wade is the best player in the country. He does the best job of combining great athleticism with the fundamentals of the game. He is a complete ballplayer."

The win was Marquette's fifth in a row over DePaul and extended its home-court winning streak to 25 straight. By this point, all four walls of the McGuire Center were up. Speculation was beginning to run rampant as to when the facility would open. In addition to the McGuire Center, a new library honoring the late Marquette President Rev. John P. Raynor was being constructed, as was a new dental school. There were a lot of changes taking place at Marquette University.

Marquette made it 26 straight when the Pirates of East Carolina invaded the Bradley Center four days later. The payback for the Dec. 30 loss was not pretty, as the Golden Eagles won 80-48. The win was a nice tune-up for Marquette as it faced its next test.

After having gone through the early-season grind of playing five out of six games on the road, the Golden Eagles entered February with a road slate that included Cincinnati, DePaul, and Louisville, and home dates with Wake Forest, Louisville, and Charlotte. This tough stretch would really show how far the team—and the program—had come under Crean.

Every game was another building block for the basketball program. The Golden Eagles' really big show at the Shoemaker Center in Cincinnati on Saturday, Feb. 1, was the game where the torch would be passed to the next powerhouse in Conference USA—Marquette. All of the games up to this point had prepared Marquette for its much anticipated match-up with the Bearcats.

In its previous seven games at the Shoe, Marquette had won just once. A level of frustration had been building among Marquette fans over the past few years. What does the team have to do to win at The Shoe over Bob Huggins? The coach, affectionately known as "Huggy Bear," had suffered a heart attack while on a recruiting trip to Pittsburgh earlier in the fall, and his courtside behavior had been watched more closely since that occurred. Huggins frustrations during the season were compounded by the fact that this edition of the Bearcats was not as good offensively as in previous seasons. Off the court problems continued to hurt the team as well.

One of the players who was making an important contribution to improving Marquette's inside game was Robert Jackson. Listed at 6'10" and 265 pounds, Crean's "aircraft carrier" needed about half of the C-USA season to adjust his style of play from the SEC, where he banged at will for 7.7 rebounds a game. In his first few Conference USA games, Jackson's physical brand of ball was causing him early foul trouble and keeping him out of games for long stretches at a time. Still, Jackson was averaging 15.4 points and 7.3 rebounds per contest.

Against Charlotte, Jackson sat for nearly 11 minutes in the first half and 8 more in the second half after getting hit with his third foul. He sat again for a few more minutes after picking up foul number four. Jackson somehow avoided a fifth foul in the game's final five minutes. During that crucial stretch, he scored 9 of Marquette's final 15 points, en route to the 67-64 win. Without him, Marquette still would not have had a win in the state of North Carolina.

"I think I've been doing a pretty good job with it," Jackson said. "I got four fouls against Charlotte and I ended up coming back and finishing the game off strong. I feel good about that. [The coaching staff] has been on me to keep my head in the game. But basically it's all focus," Jackson told Todd Rosiak, Marquette beat writer for the *Journal Sentinel*.

At the Shoemaker Center, it was Marquette's solid inside game anchored by Jackson that made the early difference. Jackson and his bookend, Merritt, blocked shots, played hard-nosed defense, and finished their put-backs solidly. There would be no intimidation on this day. The Golden Eagles were ready to move up in class and dominated this game from the get-go. Marquette—ranked 16th in the ESPN/USA TODAY poll and 18th in the AP—came into the game with a six-game winning streak, tied with Cincinnati for second in the American Division.

After Jackson made three of Marquette's four lay-ups to start the game, Wade was hit with two quick fouls. Once again, the Golden Eagles found a way to play without their star as freshman Chapman stepped up and helped extend Marquette's lead to 19-12. During the nearly seven minutes Wade sat on the bench, the team's lead had grown to 25-15. Marquette's early inside dominance surprised the denizens in the Shoemaker Center and left a visibly upset Huggins flailing on the sideline, wondering why his team was not playing hard. He was so frustrated early in the game that he pulled all five of his starters out of the game.

Marquette, remembering very clearly what had happened a year earlier, took the game to Cincinnati. Marquette was taking no prisoners, especially on the inside. The Golden Eagles took a 39-30 lead at halftime, and did not let up after the break. "They did to Cincinnati what Cincinnati did to everyone else," noted Steve "The Homer" True. Marquette's inside dominance even impressed Cincinnati legend and NBA Hall of Famer Oscar Robertson, who was the halftime guest of True and George Thompson.

At the start of the second half, a fresh Wade scored four straight baskets to keep the Bearcats' fans in their seats. After Marquette built its lead to 22 points in the second half, WISN radio play-by-play announcer Steve "The Homer" True turned to George Thompson and asked, "George, who's in the house tonight?" Answered Thompson: "Don't check until this baby is in the bag."

Sure enough, the Bearcats, behind the three-point shooting of Tony Bobbitt—and a few Marquette turnovers—narrowed the lead to eight with 2:22 left. But Marquette's outstanding free-throw shooting (first in the C-USA at 81.3 percent) sealed it. At one point, the team hit 17 straight and made 25 out of 30 for the game. Marquette showed tremendous poise as the Bearcats made their comeback. Unlike previous years, Marquette was able to withstand Cincinnati's runs and come away with a win. The victory was a statement game. Marquette showed not only that it could win in a very hostile arena, but it beat Cincinnati at its own game without resorting to thuggery. Jason Maxiell? He finished with three points. The Golden Eagles now had sole possession of second place in the American Division.

"At Cincinnati, I'm sure they realized how good they could be," said True of Marquette's performance.

Hank Raymonds was the next Marquette great to be honored as the Golden Eagles welcomed the St. Louis Billikens (Raymonds' alma mater) on Tuesday, Feb. 5. A crowd of 13,444 attended to thank the former coach for all that he had done for the program as coach, athletic director, and all-around ambassador. For the fourth time in as many games against the Billikens, Wade was held under double digits—the only team ever to do so. He had seven points, eight rebounds, four assists, three blocks, and a steal. Travis Diener had 21 to lead Marquette, followed by Jackson's 15.

The following Sunday, Feb. 9, an NCAA Tournament atmosphere permeated the Bradley Center, as the Golden Eagles welcomed the ACC's first-place Wake Forest Demon Deacons. You could flip-flop both teams' national poll rankings. Marquette was No. 14 in ESPN/USA TODAY and 15 in AP, while Wake was just the reverse in both. Marquette took an eight-game winning streak into the game, while Wake had won four in a row.

Students were standing outside the Bradley Center for well over an hour before tip-off, waiting to get their tickets. A crowd of 17,370 came to the Bradley Center, despite the frigid winter temperatures. Marquette students, clad in gold WE ARE MARQUETTE FANATICS T-shirts, extended across four sections of the arena. ABC billed the game as Wade versus 6'6" forward Josh Howard of Wake, both players leading their respective conferences in scoring, Wade at 21.9 per game and Howard at 19.2. And while both players lived up to their respective billing, it was the players around them who stood out.

In the second half, Wade stole the ball and drove for a monster dunk, recording the 1,000th point of his career. He reached the milestone in just 52 games. Only George Thompson had reached that milestone more quickly (50 games). Wade had 18 points, three rebounds, two assists, a block, and five steals, and Jackson had his fourth double-double of the season (19 points, 11 rebounds). Jackson's size and deft footwork so impressed ABC analyst Larry Conley on one play, he quipped: "When the bear goes into the woods, you'd better clear a path for him." As strong as Marquette's inside game was, the Golden Eagles were still outrebounded by Wake, 48 to 35, which matched the Demon Deacons' nation-leading rebound margin average.

But the show was almost stolen by Merritt. The junior power forward showed the country the full range of his potential at both ends of the court. He confidently scored with his patented jump hooks and showed great footwork around the basket. Toward the end of the game, he even brought out his crossover dribble and went the length of the court with the ball. It was probably the most impressive overall performance of his career. Merritt's confidence had grown exponentially from his sophomore year, when he was criticized for being soft and not fulfilling his potential.

Merritt's 16 points, nine rebounds, two blocked shots, and a steal were eye-opening, and helped lead the Golden Eagles to a 64-59 win. It was another win over a regular-season conference champion. It seemed as if Marquette was starting to make a habit of it. After the 2001–02 season, Merritt spent a great deal of time in the weight room and worked. Hard. There was no hint of the tentativeness he had shown in his first two years at Marquette. He was playing his position and playing it better than he had ever played it. His consistently improved play, so well complemented by Jackson's inside presence, made Marquette a much more dangerous team. It was not just the Dwyane Wade Show anymore for Marquette. The Golden Eagles now had a balanced, inside and outside attack. And analyst Conley predicted that Marquette (17-3) would receive anywhere from a three to a five seed in the NCAA Tournament. Wake Forest coach Skip Prosser added his own prediction: "This is a Final Four team."

During the late afternoon of Wednesday, Feb. 12, a number of buses of Marquette students left Milwaukee for the Allstate Arena in Rosemont, Illinois, to cheer on the Golden Eagles against DePaul. Dressed in gold and wearing foam cheese wedges on their heads, some dressed like Blue Man Group rejects, the Marquette fans came in force to the Allstate Arena, or as it was now being referred to: "Marquette campus South." Marquette's fans had dominated the Allstate Arena with their numbers in the last few years, especially the students who came by the busload from Milwaukee. There were concerns about Marquette letting down against the Blue Demons (who had an impressive 11-1 home record) and looking ahead

Dwyane Wade dunks for one of his 21 points against the University of South Florida at the Bradley Center, Jan. 11, which was also "George Thompson Appreciation Night."

Jackson pulls down one of his 11 rebounds against Wake Forest, a game in which he had a double-double. He also scored 19 points against the Demon Deacons.

Wade and Jackson leave the Al McGuire Court triumphantly after another home win. Marquette was 15-1 at the Bradley Center during the 2002-03 campaign, and won 31 of the 32 games over the past two seasons.

Tom Crean holds his son, Riley, and the net from one of the baskets at the Bradley Center after Marquette defeated Cincinnati for its first outright Conference USA regular season championship. Marquette defeated Cincinnati 70-61 on Senior Day, March 8, 2003.

Wade drives for one of his 22 points against Pittsburgh on Thursday, March 27, 2003, at the Metrodome. With the win, Marquette reached the Elite Eight of the NCAA Tournament for the first time since 1977.

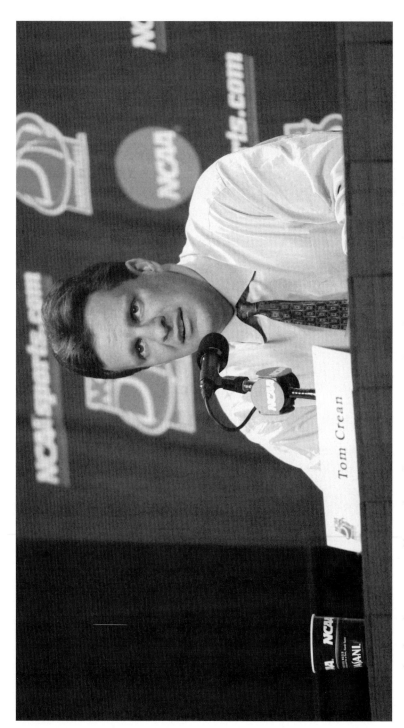

Marquette head coach Tom Crean addresses the media at a postgame question and answer session during the 2003 NCAA Tournament.

Marquette fans swarmed the Hubert H. Humphrey Metrodome in Minneapolis for the Midwest Regional Final between Kentucky and Marquette on March 29, 2003. Kentucky fans were clearly in the minority among the 28,383 fans who attended. The Metrodome was awash in a sea of gold and drowned out by the constant refrain of "WE ARE MARQUETTE!"

"Mr. Triple Double." Wade offers a rare emotional outburst after helping lead Marquette to the Final Four for the first time since '77. His 29 points, 11 rebounds and 11 assists made him only the third player in NCAA Tournament history to get a triple double, after Earvin "Magic" Johnson (Michigan State, 1979) and Andre Miller (Utah, 1998). His performance earned Wade another title: "Most Outstanding Player" in the Midwest Regional.

to Saturday's nationally-televised showdown against No. 2 Louisville, which was playing St. Louis that night.

While the Chicago media raved about Wade and looked forward to the future lottery pick's appearance, it was another Golden Eagle who would get the chance to shine on this night: freshman Steve Novak, the highest-rated recruit in Crean's stable. He matched Wade's 17-point-performance with 17 of his own on 5 of 6 shooting from three-point range. That proved to be too much for the gritty Demons to overcome as Marquette won 73-60. Marquette did get a scare late in the game when Travis Diener ran into the Blue Demons' 6'9" Sam Hoskin. Diener fell to the floor in a heap. He twisted his back and was moving gingerly the rest of the game. The sophomore had to be carried to the bus after the game. In the continuing saga of battling cousins, Travis and his other cousin, DePaul's Drake, both had seven points, but Travis had three rebounds and three assists, compared to one and none, respectively, for Drake.

During the game, word reached the Marquette bench that Louisville's 17-game winning streak was ended by St. Louis, 59-58. Marquette was now in sole possession of first place in the American Division. It was the Cardinals who let down against the tough Billikens. Marquette was now ready for the showdown of the season with the Cardinals. Dicky V was making ANOTHER appearance in Milwaukee to broadcast a Marquette game, and from all indications it was going to be another sellout.

Diener was held out of the Thursday practice because of his back injury. The team was going to give him as much rest as he needed before Saturday's Big Event. Crean and the team received some good news: Schwab had moved up to the top 10 on the organ-donor list, thus reducing the length of time he would have to wait for a lung transplant. He had also signed up as a national spokesman for organ donors.

When Crean met with ABC on Friday for its media prep of the game in a conference room on campus, he asked Vitale and play-by-play announcer Dan Schulman if they could sit in the same chairs as Vitale and Musburger had the year before, when Marquette defeated Louisville, 75-63. "He's not superstitious," Vitale laughed.

That Friday night, the Milwaukee Bucks were playing at the Bradley Center. As fans were leaving after the game, Marquette students began lining up outside the doors of the stadium just after midnight in nine-degree weather. They would camp out all night until the doors opened the next morning. The game would not begin until 2:30 p.m. that afternoon. On Saturday morning, as the students were waiting for the doors to open, they were treated to donuts, hot chocolate, and coffee. Crean had heard about their all-night vigil and decided to show his appreciation to the students for their loyalty to the team. The students were obviously surprised and grateful.

On National Marquette Day the fans set another attendance record when 18,850 crammed the Bradley Center, breaking the record set at the DePaul game the year before. The student section was solid gold once again, from top to bottom, and extended across five sections. It opened the eyes of the players when they came out for the pre-game warm-ups. It was an NCAA Tournament atmosphere as No. 11 Marquette faced No. 2 Louisville, which had won 17 games in a row before losing to St. Louis just three days before. Predicted Vitale, "These will be two dangerous teams in the postseason."

Pitino's Cardinals came out of the locker room wearing black instead of their traditional red uniforms. Louisville was 0-4 the year before when it wore black uniforms, but Pitino said he wasn't superstitious. First place in the American Division of Conference USA was at stake, as well as Marquette's 28-game winning streak at the Bradley Center. Who was in the house for the game? None other than Denny Crum, who was the Cardinals' coach the last time Marquette had lost a game at Al McGuire Court, two years before.

The fast-paced start had both teams in transition, and almost every shot was contested. Vitale hyped the match-up of Wade ("Baryshnikov in shorts") and Madison, Wisconsin, native Reece Gaines as his "Rolls Royce Backcourt." Vitale, complimenting both coaches, asked at least twice during the broadcast: "Will they [Marquette] be able to keep Crean?"

Marquette was well prepared for Louisville's press. Crean had seven players attacking the starting five in his Friday afternoon practice session. Vitale said that *New York Daily News* basketball writer Dick "Hoops" Weiss told him it was the most "intense practice the day before a game he had seen."

In the back-and-forth action, neither team led by more than six points. Marquette led at the half 36-35. The Golden Eagles were led by freshman

Steve Novak's 11 points. Wade was having a tough time from the field, and while Diener was trying to play through the pain, he was not himself. Pitino took advantage of Diener's injured back by sticking 6'6" freshman Francisco Garcia on the tough but hobbled 6-foot Diener.

As the teams went through numerous ties and lead changes, the noise became "deafening," according to ABC's Schulman, who added that the game was heading toward "a fantastic finish." The students had been standing all game, and with 5:22 remaining it was tied for the 16th time. Neither of these well-matched teams deserved to lose this game. It was one of those back-and-forth contests that would go to the team that had the ball last.

Louisville's Ellis Myles, who had 14 rebounds, sank two free throws to give the Cardinals a 70-67 lead. Marquette at one point had hit 18 straight free throws, and missed just one out of 22 for the game.

With 29.6 seconds remaining, everyone in the Bradley Center was out of their seats, and not just the students. Diener put up a long, contested three-pointer that rattled in with just 11.3 seconds left. That tied the game and sent the Bradley Center faithful into full roar. Bad back and all, Diener's clutch shot showed his toughness and ability to play through the pain.

Louisville's Gaines brought the ball up court, with Wade guarding him. As Wade backpedaled toward the three-point arc, Gaines quickly stopped just beyond NBA range and fired off a long jumper. It seemed that he pulled the trigger too quickly, but the shot went in to give the Cardinals a three-point lead, 73-70, with 5.5 seconds left, silencing the sold-out crowd that just seconds earlier was in full throat when Diener's shot fell in.

After a time-out, Marquette quickly brought the ball up court, Diener dribbled it into the front court, but did not see an open Novak on the right side. Diener put up a tough shot with Garcia in his face, but it fell short. Louisville snapped Marquette's home-court winning streak, but came away with a respect for the Golden Eagles that they did not have when they celebrated on the Bradley Center floor after winning the triple-overtime game two years earlier. In the Rolls Royce Backcourt report, Wade finished 3 of 13 for 15 points, while Gaines finished with 20 after having scored just four in the first half. And Marquette outrebounded Louisville, 41-38.

It was a game that lived up to the hype, and easily could have gone either way. That is how close and well matched the two teams were on that afternoon. During ABC's post-game report, Digger Phelps reminded viewers that Marquette was heading to Freedom Hall in 12 days for the rematch. "They ain't done yet."

Marquette could very well have folded up its tent and gone into a funk after the game, but it did not. Before its Thursday night game against UNC–Charlotte at the Bradley Center, the team learned that Louisville had lost to Memphis at Freedom Hall, which put the Golden Eagles back in first place. While Diener's sore back was still a concern, his rehab was coming along.

Coaches do not ordinarily become icons after just a few years on the job. Especially if they have not won any championships. But nowadays, when a coach gets a bobblehead doll made in his image, that is a sure sign that he has made it. The Charlotte game was "Tom Crean Bobblehead Night," and some 5,000 of the dolls were given away to fans. According to Todd Rosiak's story in the *Journal Sentinel,* Crean "felt a little uncomfortable with it at first, but to see it and have people respond to it, it's a great honor." Crean also wished that his children "weren't so afraid of it when they see it. To think that my bobblehead would be on e-Bay, that's a humbling thing."

Dwyane Wade had 21 points and nine rebounds to lead four players in double figures, and Merritt had a double-double (11 points, 10 rebounds) as Marquette, with a 75-67 victory, completed a season sweep over Charlotte for the first time EVER. Diener added 12 points on four of six shooting, including two of three from three-point range in 28 minutes. Not bad for a guy with a sore back.

Marquette then won its sixth straight road game, defeating TCU in Ft. Worth 79-68. Crean took the road game as an opportunity to introduce an NCAA Tournament feel to the road trip, with a strict time schedule for film study, practice, and travel, according to Todd Rosiak's game story in the *Journal Sentinel.*

It seemed that the team was getting this road trip stuff down pretty well, as it prepared for its rematch with Louisville in five days at Freedom Hall. Once again, Vitale would be on hand to broadcast this showdown between two teams vying for first place in Conference USA's American Division.

The Golden Eagles were heading into the rematch ranked 10th in the AP and 11th in the ESPN/USA TODAY polls, while Louisville had dropped from No. 2 in the country to No. 11 in the AP poll. A cloud hung over the game, as the NCAA was investigating Louisville center Marvin Stone's high school background. He was expected to play against Marquette, however.

The rivalry between the teams had become more competitive over the previous several years, with games being decided on buzzer-beaters and in overtime. There were more than 20,000 fans at Freedom Hall and they were loud, but the Golden Eagles were not daunted.

The Cardinals jumped all over the Golden Eagles right from the opening tip, forcing turnovers, bad shots, bad passes, and just plain bad basketball. It seemed as if Marquette could not do anything right in the first half. Marquette committed 14 turnovers that half (18 for the game) and trailed Louisville by as many as 19 points. It looked bleak.

After getting settled, Marquette slowly chipped away at the lead, however, cutting the deficit by halftime to 46-35. Before the team went into the locker room, Crean huddled the players on the court and gave them a pep talk.

Whatever it was that he said, it worked. After five minutes were gone in the second half, the Louisville lead was cut to six. With just over 11 minutes left in the game, the game was tied at 61. A Merritt jumper put Marquette ahead, 63-61, with just under 10 minutes left in the regulation.

It was at this point that Wade, who had scored nine points in the first half, took charge. He scored 19 points in the second half on 9 of 17 shooting, and added eight rebounds and seven assists. Merritt had 18 points and Diener 16. Robert Jackson was really not a factor for one of the few times all season, finishing with just four points.

After the Cardinals took a 65-64 lead, Marquette went on another run, building a lead of 72-67. The team kept Louisville at bay with free throws the rest of the way, hitting 21 of 29 for the game, while the Cardinals could manage only 15 of 30. They missed some key free throws down the stretch.

With just over a minute left, Ellis Myles fell awkwardly on a player's foot and went down with a torn patella tendon in his right knee. Pitino's flushed expression said it all, as he watched his young star, who had a double-double (12 points, 11 rebounds), get helped off the court.

Reece Gaines had a chance to be the hero once again, with Marquette up 76-73. With just seconds left, he put up a three-pointer that would not go, and the Golden Eagles left a shocked Freedom Hall crowd with its 21st win against four losses (12-2 Conference USA). More important, it was Marquette's seventh straight road win, improving to 7-3 from 5-5 the year before. Louisville dropped to 19-5, and the loss seemed to sap its momentum. After streaking to a 17-0 record, it had lost to St. Louis, Memphis, Cincinnati, and Marquette. Freshman Francisco Garcia led the Cardinals with 24 points on 9 of 18 shooting.

The win was being described as the best in Crean's four-year tenure in Milwaukee. In George Thompson's words, the game was a "Wang Dang Doodle." Once again, it was another step up, another brick in the foundation, a gut-check game that gave the team a confidence boost for the rest of the season. It seemed that this team believed it could do anything it set its mind to. Just like its young coach had drawn it up.

Next up was UAB at the Bradley Center. A win would secure the Golden Eagles at least a share of the Conference USA title—Marquette's first. Another sellout crowd of 18,315 came to cheer their heroes home after the exciting win at Louisville.

UAB, coming in with a 16-8 record (8-5 C-USA), was not there to cheer on old Marquette, however. First-year coach Mike Anderson's Blazers came to win. During the season, UAB forced 22 turnovers a game, in addition to getting 12 steals. Anderson, a longtime assistant to former Arkansas coach Nolan Richardson, was a disciple of Richardson's "40 minutes of hell," which Anderson had incorporated into UAB's up-tempo style of play.

Marquette led 50-42 at the half, and extended it to a seemingly comfortable 20-point margin with under seven minutes to play. The Blazers, however, looking like Richardson's old Razorbacks, used their press to cut the lead to eight, with about three minutes left. Marquette made 10 of 12 free throws down the stretch (33 of 37 overall) to seal the 98-87 win. Crean and Anderson exchanged a warm embrace at the end of the game.

After the Louisville game, Marquette was drained, both emotionally and physically. And it looked it, at times, as UAB forced the action. While Marquette won, it was not pretty. Marquette had five players in double figures, led by Wade's 26 points. In addition to his seven assists, four steals, and four blocked shots, there was one statistic that he would probably like to forget: eight turnovers. The team had 21 total, the worst of the season.

While many fans that night did not seem overly concerned, the team had committed 39 turnovers in its last two games, not a good trend as tournament time approached.

The team was looking forward to Senior Day, March 8, when Marquette would close out the regular season by beating Cincinnati and winning the team's first outright Conference USA title. Crean wanted his players to be able to call themselves outright conference champions for the first time. And the team would get its chance to dethrone the seven-time defending conference champion Bearcats. It would be the last game Marquette would play at the Bradley Center before the post-season.

After the wins, Marquette moved up to No. 8 in the country in both the AP and ESPN/USA TODAY polls. It was the highest a Marquette team had been ranked since March 13, 1978, during Hank Raymonds' first year as head coach. The previous season, Crean's Crew finished at No. 9 in the country. Throughout the season, Marquette had steadily moved up in the rankings among the nation's elite teams. While Crean was pleased with the rankings, he did not want the players to take anything for granted. There was more work to be done. And not just for the upcoming game.

On March 3 of that week, Crean set aside time for the players to prepare for the game sets of both Arizona and Kentucky, the top two teams in the country. It was another way of getting the players to believe that they would probably be playing these two teams at some point in the NCAA Tournament.

Wade was also named Conference USA Player of the Week for the fifth time that season, after averaging 27 points, 5.5 rebounds, 7 assists, 3 blocked shots, and 2.5 steals in Marquette's wins over Louisville and UAB. Wade was mentioned among those vying for National Player of the Year, along with Texas' T.J. Ford, Xavier's David West, Kansas' Nick Collison, Oklahoma's Hollis Price, and Wake Forest's Josh Howard. Wade was also still in the running for the Wooden, Naismith, and Robertson awards.

Early in the Cincinnati game, the Golden Eagles were out of sync, hitting just one of their first six shots. The sea of gold in the student section was waiting for something to scream about, but Marquette just seemed off its game. Cincinnati was getting good looks and hitting its shots, especially from three-point range, where the Bearcats were 6 of 11. Marquette had none in four attempts, and seemed to be staying close by getting to the free-throw line.

Even though Cincinnati had a slim lead at the half (33-29), and was 17-1 during the season in games where they led at the half, Wade continued his dominance before the fourth sellout (18,790) of the season. His 26 points, 10 rebounds, five assists, three blocks, and three steals helped Marquette win its first outright Conference USA title over Cincinnati 70-61.

Wade put on an unforgettable show, scoring points on spin moves, with kisses off the glass, dunks, and alley-oops. But that was just on the offensive end. On one sequence at the 13:50 mark of the second half, Wade missed a tip-in, ran the length of the court, jumped up and blocked Eric Hicks' shot back into Hicks as the players flew out of bounds. Marquette ball. At the other end, Diener spotted Wade at liftoff, threw an alley-oop that forced Wade to readjust in mid-air and reach back for the ball, and he still laid it in for two points. By that point everyone in the Bradley Center was on their feet, students and the longtime alums and fans sporting the gold sweater vests that Crean helped make fashionable.

Wade's play at both ends was a great example of hustle, leaping ability, hang time, and change of direction. It was Jordanesque. He also knew how to get to the free-throw line, averaging at least 10 free throws a game in the previous five games. But it was Wade's steals, blocks, and passes that had everyone talking, including ABC announcers Terry Gannon and Jay Bilas.

"When your best player is your hardest worker, it is a joy for a coach," noted Bilas. When Wade fell out of bounds after hitting a fallaway jumper, Gannon exclaimed, "Dwyane Wade is making every big play, getting every big shot here in the second half for Marquette." "And getting every big rebound," added Bilas. "There is not a column on the stat sheet where Wade does not have a 3 or a 4."

Wade was ably assisted by the team's only senior on this day, Robert Jackson, who put Marquette ahead for the first time in the game at the 17:01 mark of the second half, and had a solid 17 points and nine rebounds. Scott Merritt added 12 points, four rebounds, and four assists, and Diener had 10 points, including two of four from three-point range—both in the second half. Diener also was hit in the midsection, which forced him to the bench holding his chest. Wade took over at the point, and Marquette kept Cincinnati from hitting a field goal for the last three and a half minutes of the game.

As well as Cincinnati shot in the first half, they shot that poorly in the second half, hitting just one of seven at one point and missing four free throws during that stretch. Cincinnati could get no closer than three points. Freshman Tony Bobbitt led the Bearcats with 13 points, followed by Armein Kirkland with 11, Leonard Stokes 10, and Taron Barker with nine. Jason Maxiell scored eight for Cincinnati, but he was not a factor. Marquette out-rebounded Cincinnati by 17 in their first meeting, and won the battle of the boards again, 36-23.

The Golden Eagles also secured the top seed in the conference tournament in Louisville. It was the first time in the eight-year history of the conference that Cincinnati was not the No. 1 seed in the tournament. Cincinnati received a No. 5 seed, marking the first time ever the team would be forced to play on the first day of the C-USA tournament.

The students and fans spilled onto the court, embracing the players and the beaming Coach Crean, as blue, gold, and silver confetti fell from the ceiling of the Bradley Center. It looked like a coronation, but it was really a big thank-you for one memorable season in which 246,844 fans came through the turnstiles for a per-game average of 15,553—good enough for 11th best in the country. Students were dancing and jumping up and down with delight. Merritt held aloft a sign that read C-USA CHAMPION, and Wade signaled No. 1 with his index finger. The players, coaches, and fans partied together for more than half an hour, until the trophy presentation and the Senior Day honors for Jackson.

Now, they could call themselves CHAMPIONS. Conference champions for the first time since the 1993–94 Warriors won the old Great Midwest Conference. The win was a huge building block for the Marquette basketball program. In the post-game press conference, Crean was appreciative and thankful to everyone involved in the program, athletically and academically, and ceded the interview stage to his assistants: Jeff Strohm, Trey Schwab, Darrin Horn, and Steven Giles. One championship down, one more to go, reminded Wade.

The roof was now in place on the McGuire Center. And visitors to the site who did not know any better would think that the old MECCA was lifted up and dropped down right on Wells Street. The McGuire Center looks like a modern version of the old Milwaukee Arena where Coach Al built the foundation for Marquette's winning ways. The design, whether intentional or accidental, is a fitting tribute.

The team could now concentrate on preparing for its next game in Louisville. Crean had new T-shirts made up with "0-0" on the back, to let the players know it was a new season, and they could not rest on their newly won laurels.

When the team began its practices at Freedom Hall, there was no let-up by the players. It was full tilt, just like at the Old Gym. It was during the workouts that the Conference USA awards were announced, in front of the players, families, and Coach Crean's family.

Wade was named to the Conference First Team, and was Defensive Player of the Year and Player of the Year. Crean won the Ray Meyer Award as Coach of the Year for the second straight time. Only Huggins had won it two years running in Conference USA. Steve Novak was named to the All Freshman Team and was selected Sixth Man of the Year, while Travis Diener was named 2nd Team All Conference with his averages of 11.2 points, 5.7 assists, and 3.2 rebounds a game.

As well as Marquette was playing, there was speculation that it could garner a number-one seed in the NCAA Tournament by winning the Conference USA tourney, and no less than a two seed by making the title game. In fact, *Sports Illustrated* predicted in its weekly seeding report that Marquette would get a one seed. The Golden Eagles had defeated regular-season conference champions Wisconsin (Big Ten) and Wake Forest (ACC), won the regular season C-USA, and had an impressive road record (7-3), including tough wins at Cincinnati and Louisville, as well as sweeping Charlotte.

In addition to the road record, the improvements Marquette made in conference play since Crean took over were stunning: No. 1 in field goal percent (48.5%), free throw percentage (76.5%; highest since Marquette's national champions' 77.8%), three-point field goal percentage (37.7%), and assists-to-turnover ratio (1.27 to 1). Its average of 78.5 points per game was the highest since the 1970–71 Warriors averaged 81.7 a game. Simply stated, Marquette had taken care of business during the regular season. It had won 15 of its last 16 games, the last loss coming at home to Louisville on

Feb. 15. The Golden Eagles' 23-4 record marked the second straight year with 20 or more wins, the first time since the 1996–97 and 1997–98 seasons under Deane. Marquette also had a 14-2 record in the conference and an RPI of 7. At worst, the speculation was that the team would earn a No. 3 seed and play close to home at the RCA Dome in Indianapolis for its first- and second-round games.

But first things first. The team had business to take care of in Louisville. Crean did a good job of getting his players to focus on the task at hand throughout the season. As cliched as Crean's "one-game-at-a-time" philosophy sounded, he kept everything simple for his players. What he was trying to communicate to his players was, after all, not complicated. Crean's goal each weekend of the post-season was to win a championship. The C-USA Tournament was the first. The first opponent was UAB, in a rematch of the March 1 game at the Bradley Center. The Blazers nearly embarrassed the Golden Eagles in Milwaukee. Marquette was the favorite to not only win its opening-round game, but the tournament championship.

At Freedom Hall, UAB took it to Marquette once again. This time, the Blazers forced 30 turnovers (a C-USA tourney record) with their tenacious press, Marquette's worst performance of the season. Ten of those were committed by Wade (an individual tourney record), who scored just 11 points. UAB's up-tempo style also resulted in 20 steals (another tournament record) for the Blazers. It was the third of four games in which Marquette committed turnovers in high double digits.

Diener kept Marquette's hopes alive with 19 points on sharp three-point shooting, but turnovers by Robert Jackson (18 points) and Wade did the team in. There were no excuses after the 83-76 loss, but the game showed the team it needed to concentrate on the task at hand if it expected to advance very far in the post-season. All of the individual honors that Crean and the players received could not take away the pain and embarrassment of that loss. It was back to Milwaukee to get back to work and start again at 0-0.

While not getting a chance to play for the tournament title, the team did have a chance to refocus, rest, and get ready for the NCAA Tournament. In the final polls of the season, Marquette dropped to No. 9 in AP and No. 11 in ESPN/USA TODAY. Also, the team's RPI dropped from 7 to 13.

During an appearance on Chicago's ESPN Radio 1000, ESPN analyst Jay Bilas was asked by a caller whether it was possible for Marquette to get to the Final Four. "With the right seeding, getting placed in the right region, and getting some breaks along the way, sure it is possible for Marquette to get to the Final Four."

Two days after returning from Louisville, Crean gathered his players and coaches in a private room at TGIFriday's at Miller Park to watch CBS' "Selection Sunday" telecast, just as they had the year before. Crean's penchant for following a set routine extended even to these kinds of events. Even though the team had lost badly to UAB the previous Thursday, Crean believed that Marquette still had a chance of getting a No. 1 seed because of its solid body of work during the regular season.

As the team settled in at TGIFriday's, they waited for CBS' Greg Gumbel to announce the Midwest Region pairings. The nation's top-ranked team, Kentucky, was the No. 1 seed and Marquette was No. 3. The last time Marquette received a seed as high as 3 was in 1979, the first year the NCAA began the seeding process for the tournament. It was a nice improvement over the previous season's No. 5 seed. And one of the privileges of a high seed is a nice hotel.

The 23-5 Golden Eagles were in good company at number 3. Others included Duke (West Region), Xavier (South), and Syracuse (East). And the Golden Eagles were also playing very close to home, with its first round game set for the RCA Dome in Indianapolis against the No. 14 seed Holy Cross, another Jesuit school. The Crusaders, winners of the Patriot League title, were coached by one of Crean's mentors, Ralph Willard. This history brought up the teacher-versus-student angle for the 11:20 a.m. first-round match on Thursday, March 20.

Selection Sunday was a good day for Wisconsin teams, as three were placed in the Midwest Regional. Marquette's instate nemesis and Big Ten regular-season champ, Wisconsin, earned a No. 5 seed and was to meet No. 12 Weber State in Spokane. And for the first time ever, UW–Milwaukee, winner of the Horizon League crown and led by second-year coach Bruce Pearl, was invited to the Big Dance. The Panthers, a No. 12 seed, would face No. 5 Notre Dame in its first-round match, also in Indianapolis.

"It says a lot about the individual programs, the universities," Crean told Rosiak of the *Journal Sentinel*. "It says a lot about how kids are being coached in high school and in the summertime, and how the fans are supporting the programs. So many people are gaining an appreciation for what the programs in this state do, and I don't think it should stop with the Division I programs. Look at what UW–Stevens Point continues to do, and all the programs in this state. I think it says a lot. It's such a great sports state."

Also in the Midwest Regional were the Big East Champion Pittsburgh Panthers, who, when they were shown watching CBS' coverage after earning a No. 2 seed, seemed rather nonchalant about the whole thing. CBS analyst Bill Raftery said, "C'mon guys, show a little excitement!" Joining them were Missouri, Southern Illinois, Indiana, Illinois, and Alabama. CBS's analysts, including Raftery, Clark Kellogg, Jim Nantz, and Billy Packer, considered the Midwest the weakest of the four regions. All thought that Kentucky, with its 23-game winning streak, had the easiest road to New Orleans. "The Wildcats have an excellent chance to win it all in New Orleans," declared Kellogg.

Packer and Nantz spent a good deal of their air time complaining to Tournament Chairman and Arizona AD Jim Livengood that Arizona and Kentucky should not have been on the same side of the bracket, forcing a potential national semifinal game instead of the teams possibly meeting for the national championship. Livengood noted that the committee was not in the business of predicting which teams would be advancing or envisioning Final Four scenarios, though Packer insisted it was the committee's responsibility. Packer then asked when the committee would consider reseeding teams at the Final Four. Livengood noted that it was not a question considered by the committee. Packer and Nantz also complained that Illinois should have received a No. 2 seed. It was Packer who, when asked late in the season which "mid-major" conference would get four bids, responded, "Conference USA." This irked a number of the conference's backers, including member coaches. CBS received at least a dozen phone calls complaining about Packer's comments. Memphis and Cincinnati, number 7 and 8 seeds, respectively, in the West, and Louisville (No. 4 seed East), were the three teams joining Marquette from Conference USA.

Marquette was headed to the Big Dance for the second straight year. The last time that happened was during the 1995–96 and 1996–97 seasons. The next day *Sports Illustrated*'s NCAA Preview would be released, with the prominent players, coaches, teams, and announcers in a cover collage. A photo of Wade appeared in the lower right-hand corner of the March 24, 2003, cover. But there really was no need to worry about the *SI* Cover Jinx. There were just too many other players depicted on the cover. *SI*'s prediction for the Golden Eagles: Marquette beats Holy Cross and then loses to Missouri in the second round.

The difference for Marquette was that a lack of tournament experience was not going to be a factor. After having gone through the disappointment of losing in the first round of its conference tournament, the team's focus was clearly on the task at hand: Taking the Road to the Final Four and New Orleans. Even with five players returning from last year's tournament squad—Wade, Townsend, Merritt, Diener, and Sanders—the Road to the Big Easy would not be easy.

The *Chicago Tribune*'s Skip Myslenski dubbed this bunch of Golden Eagles "Dwyane and the Dingoes" in a story before the first round. A dingo is a wild dog, and Myslenski compared the team's play to a pack of wild dogs. "Marquette plays rabidly, tenaciously, with the ferocity of an attacking pack, always yipping and yapping, always scratching and clawing aside its superb leader, the multitalented Dwyane Wade." He also gave special mention to Townsend, noting that the sophomore played a number of roles for the team, from stopping the opposing team's best player with his hard-nosed defense to hitting the clutch three-pointer when it was needed.

The Golden Eagles' first-round opponent, Holy Cross, boasted an experienced squad, having won three straight Patriot League titles and appeared in three straight NCAA Tournaments. As a No. 16 seed in 2002, Holy Cross lost to Kansas by 11, and in 2000 as a No. 15 seed lost to Kentucky by just four points. The Crusaders had four players averaging in double figures. While Holy Cross could not match up with Marquette's quickness, it did have a front line of 6'10" Patrick Whearty and 6'8" Tim Szatko to battle Jackson and Merritt. In reserve was former North Carolina transfer Neil Fingleton at 7'6".

During the team's last practice at the Old Gym before heading for Indianapolis, it received some bad news. Diener was suffering from shin splints in his right leg. He was held out of practice and getting rehabbed before the team left Milwaukee.

Marquette prepared for the Crusaders' match-up and 1-3-1 zones, and also worked on protecting the basketball, which was a serious problem for the team late in the season.

As the players boarded their bus outside of the Old Gym on a cold Tuesday afternoon, March 18, a number of students were there to see them off on the next leg of their fantastic journey to join the elite of college basketball: Indianapolis. Little did they know where this journey would eventually lead. ▪

CHAPTER FOUR:
MARCH TO MADNESS

arch Madness, the time of year with brackets, pools, and the excitement students and college basketball fans feel about their teams, really takes hold of the country for two weeks every spring.

This season, however, there were clouds on the horizon. A number of Villanova players were caught using an access code to make long-distance phone calls. St. Bonaventure was banned from playing in the Atlantic 10 postseason tournament, when it was learned that it had played an ineligible player (Jamil Terrell) during the season. The players then decided to boycott the team's last two regular season games, which started a firestorm that resulted in the eventual firing or resignations of the basketball coach (Jan van breda Kolff), assistant coach (Kort Wickenheiser), athletic director (Gothard Lane), and university president (Robert Wickenheiser). Georgia's Jim Harrick and his son, Jim Jr., were forced to resign after being charged with academic fraud and providing improper benefits to a player. The school also decided it would not participate in the SEC and NCAA tournaments. And academic fraud within the Fresno State basketball program forced the school into a self-imposed one-year postseason ban on the team. Steve Lavin was fired at UCLA and Matt Doherty was forced out at North Carolina after difficult seasons, beginning a fierce media watch of the coaching carousel and speculation of how the coaching dominoes would fall after the tournament.

On top of all this was the uncertainty as to when the United States would invade Iraq. President Bush had given Saddam Hussein an ultimatum to leave

Iraq within 48 hours even as U.S. troops had moved into the Gulf for nearly a month. And it was not certain when the bombing of Baghdad would begin. When the war did begin there was certain to be continuous coverage on the major networks, including CBS, which has a multi-billion dollar investment in the NCAA Tournament. Contingency plans by CBS, which is owned by Viacom, called for the games to be shown on some of its other properties, including TNN, TV LAND, VH1, UPN, BET, CMT, and MTV, causing fans everywhere to cry out: "I want my NCAA!" Not too many fans were happy with the prospect of having Dan Rather's "America At War" cut-ins at crunch time of big games.

The network did consider the prospect of having ESPN air the games in the event CBS went to wall-to-wall coverage of the war. Another problem that presented was that ESPN had already committed to the NCAA Women's Tournament. If it had the men's tournament as well, ESPN would be forced to juggle its schedule in order to handle both events.

With time running out before the Tuesday, March 18, play-in game in Dayton, OH, between the tournament's two lowest seeds, UNC–Asheville and Texas Southern, NCAA President Myles Brand met with Tom Ridge, secretary of the recently-created cabinet post of Homeland Security. President Brand was concerned not only about safety considerations but whether it was even appropriate for the games to go on during the war. Marquette's Diener had a personal stake in the proceedings because his cousin, Derek, was going to be shipped out to the conflict. Brand announced after consulting with Secretary Ridge that the games would go on as scheduled, without any interruption.

In the event of a conflict between war coverage and the games, CBS did make a deal with ESPN to take over coverage of the games. It was the first time competing networks agreed to such an arrangement, but this was a special case.

MARQUETTE 72, HOLY CROSS 68

With all of this taking place, the 2002–03 edition of the Marquette Golden Eagles started their tournament march as a long-shot underdog for the NCAA title. Depending on what Las Vegas sports book you consulted, Marquette was anywhere from a 35-1 to 50-1 to win the national championship.

After the pairings were announced, Marquette's ticket allotment was sold out before the team bus left for the airport. Those who wanted the $135 all-session tickets would have to try Ticketmaster or the RCA Dome ticket office. Marquette fans were excited, but a little concerned about the first-round matchup. Besides the teacher-versus-student story angle, Holy Cross was an experienced NCAA Tournament team that gave scares to Kansas and Kentucky in previous tournaments. The Crusaders came into the tournament with a 12-game winning streak, having won 20 of their previous 21 games. Holy Cross' last loss was on Jan. 26 to American University.

Willard had a tournament-tested team, while Crean did not. Willard had won a number of NCAA Tournament games at different schools, but Crean had yet to win his first. As an assistant to Willard at Western Kentucky, Crean helped the 1992–93 Hilltoppers make the Sweet 16 with a 26-6 record. And one of the key players on that team was now a Crean assistant, Darrin Horn. So, the connections ran deep between Willard and Crean. Even the wives— Joani Crean and Dottie Willard—were e-mail pals. Crean said that he looked at Willard as a second father. With all of those mixed emotions, it was easy to see that this Vatican Championship would not be easy.

The pressure was most certainly on Marquette and Crean to get the first-round monkey off their backs so that they could concentrate on the task ahead.

The Golden Eagles were a 10- to 12-point favorite against Holy Cross, depending on the betting line. But it would be the only game in which Marquette was a favorite during its tournament run. The sports media were all over themselves looking for upsets to pick, and the Marquette game was one of them. Even the *New York Times* weighed in with its pick of Holy Cross.

In the team's Wednesday practice at the RCA Dome, Diener was not pushing it with his shin splints. He was taking it easy. It was obvious that he was not anywhere near 100 percent, but there was no way Diener was not going to play. He was determined to play, no matter what.

It was not until a few minutes before 11 a.m. on Thursday that the Marquette faithful found out the Marquette-Holy Cross game was the first casualty of the War in Iraq. It was moved to ESPN from CBS as the first bombs from the U.S. and the "coalition of the willing" began falling on Baghdad.

"Part of me wanted to stay focused on the NCAA Tournament," noted Marquette senior Jaci Pabst, "because it was positive. I had friends who were shipped over there. Five were shipped out. One was in Afghanistan. I kept looking at the casualty lists.

"We had our time when we focused on Iraq, and then when we focused on the NCAA Tournament. You had to separate them. You learn how to separate things in life. When news cut-ins came on, some students said, 'I don't need to see this now,'" noted Pabst.

As expected, the game was tough. Holy Cross' match-up zone befuddled the Golden Eagles, as Robert Jackson reverted to his foul-prone ways of earlier in the season, scoring just two points in the first half. Dwyane Wade had no points and four turnovers. Not a very auspicious start for Marquette.

It was boy-wonder Diener who carried the day for the Golden Eagles, with some clutch three-point shooting. He scored 17 of Marquette's 29 first half points on 6 of 9 shooting from the floor, including three of five from three-point land, giving the fairly good-sized Marquette contingent something to cheer about. "We had thousands of Marquette fans at the game," noted photographer John Baker. "We were reasonably well represented in the RCA Dome."

Diener showed during the season that he could hit the clutch shot, and he did so consistently against Holy Cross. Even though Jackson and Wade were not on, Diener was, and kept Marquette in the game.

While this was Holy Cross's third straight NCAA Tournament, the basketball program had not won an NCAA Tournament game since 1953. The Crusaders were threatening to change that by taking advantage of the solid inside work they were getting from Szatko (16 points), Nick Lufkin (13), and Whearty (12). The white-head-banded Crusaders outscored Marquette in the paint, 32-18, and kept pounding it inside.

Diener, whose only concession to the shin splints was a white sleeve over his leg, did not look any worse for the wear as he helped the Golden Eagles build a 28-16 lead. The Crusaders cut the lead to 29-24, with a nice 8-1 run to close out the first half.

Holy Cross picked up where it left off in the second half, hitting seven of its first 10 shots to go up 40-39. The Crusaders complemented their strong inside game with five three-pointers in the game.

The turning point of the game may have come with just over six minutes remaining and Holy Cross up 56-54. Freshman Joe Chapman hit probably the biggest three-pointer of his young career to give the Golden Eagles a 57-56 lead.

"The biggest shot of the NCAA Tournament was Joe Chapman's three-pointer against Holy Cross in that first game," insisted WISN Radio's Steve "The Homer" True.

While Wade and Diener continued to take turns making big shots in the game's final few minutes, Holy Cross refused to go away, answering with its own clutch shots.

With a minute left and Marquette up 64-62, Crean used one of his set plays out of a time-out, in which Wade set a nice screen for Diener, who was ready to shoot when he received the ball from Wade, and nailed a shot just inside the three-point line. Marquette 66, Holy Cross 62.

After trading baskets, Szatko hit a three-pointer with 12 seconds left to make it 68-65, but that was as close as the game would get. Marquette won the Vatican Championship 72-68 to up its record to 24-5 and advance to the second round for the first time since 1996. It earned a second-round date with the Missouri Tigers, who had barely defeated Southern Illinois on a last-second play, 72-71. Missouri finished fifth in the Big 12. Holy Cross was the third conference champion Marquette defeated in 2002–2003.

The 6'1" 165-pound Diener finished with a career-high 29 points in 35 minutes. He shot 9 of 14 from the floor, including 5 of 9 from three-point range, six of seven from the free-throw line. Wade was the only other Golden Eagle in double figures with 15, on just four of 11 from the field. However, as he had done all season, he contributed in other ways, with four assists, two blocked shots, and two steals, and was perfect from the free-throw line, making all seven of his shots. He did have five turnovers for the game. Wade revealed later that he had been suffering from a nagging groin injury, that had hindered him in recent games.

The difference really was at the free-throw line, where Marquette was 19 of 23 and Holy Cross was 15 of 25.

Marquette survived a tough game and was able to get the first-round monkey off its back. "After the Holy Cross game, the monkey was dead," Baker stated. "The Holy Cross game was basically the beginning. They could have found a way to lose that game," noted the *Journal Sentinel*'s Rosiak.

For Crean, while he was happy for his players, it was the first time he had coached against one of his mentors and had a difficult time personally savoring the win. His feelings of ambivalence were genuine because of the feelings he had for Willard. It is also one of the reasons Crean has not scheduled games against teams like Michigan State and his other mentor/friend Tom Izzo, and most likely will not schedule games against teams now coached by his former assistants.

Back at the team hotel in the Embassy Suites, Crean and Hank Raymonds shared a private interlude outside the entrance, which Crean did not want interrupted by a photograph. "Can we hold the pictures for right now?" Crean politely asked Baker, who let Crean have his moment with Coach Raymonds. "He handled it nicely," Baker recalled. "To him it was a personal moment, and I respected that."

Diener, the star, also brought some perspective to the post-game briefing, reminding the assembled that what his cousin Derek was doing in Iraq was much more important than what he was doing for Marquette. As *Chicago Tribune* columnist Mike Downey described Diener: ". . . a sharp shooter and an even sharper kid." In his "Downey's 11," he noted that it was "patriotic to cheer for Marquette."

Later on, however, at the post-game reception, Diener grabbed a bull-horn and confidently told the assembled Marquette faithful, "Book your trip to New Orleans," much to the delighted surprise of everyone. Diener was not only able to take the bull by the horns on the court, but off the court as well. He had established himself as a leader during the season, but his performance on this biggest of stages secured it.

After the first-round win, Crean had received a number of telephone messages at his hotel. The one he reportedly kept was from Gen. Hal Moore, one of the inspirational speakers he had talk to his team during the season. Gen. Moore's message: "Tell the troops they have to believe."

The team and coaching staff then began preparing for the Missouri Tigers, led by 36-year-old Quin Snyder, one of the coaches who interviewed for the Marquette job.

Also that first Thursday of the tournament, No. 5 Wisconsin defeated 12th-seeded Weber State 81-74, to advance to a Saturday date with the No. 13 seed Tulsa Golden Hurricane. The No. 12 seed UW–Milwaukee faced No. 5 seed Notre Dame in Indianapolis. While very few people gave the Panthers a chance to win with Notre Dame's experience, Bruce Pearl's players stayed within their game plan all night and played tenacious defense. With just a few seconds remaining, UW–Milwaukee, trailing by one point, had the ball—and the right play. After working the clock down to a previous few seconds, Dylan Page could not hit the gimme, and Notre Dame escaped with a nervous—and lucky—70-69 win. The loss did not diminish the great season the Panthers had enjoyed or the outstanding coaching job that Pearl did.

MARQUETTE 101, MISSOURI 92 (OVERTIME)

At the end of their Friday night shoot-around, the Marquette players began lining up to take last-second shots as well as half-court shots, trying to simulate game-ending situations. Novak did not fare especially well. In fact, the freshman said that he did not hit any three-point shots at the end of the workout.

The winner of the No. 3 versus No. 6-seed game would earn a trip to Minneapolis and the Sweet 16. In its Thursday first-round game, Missouri just did defeat Southern Illinois University, 72-71. Tigers' junior Rickey Paulding drove the lane and was met by the Salukis' star Jermaine Dearman, who was called for a blocking foul. It was a call that could have gone either way; Paulding could have been called for a charge. But Paulding went to the line and hit his second free throw to give the Tigers the controversial win.

Before the Golden Eagles faced the Tigers, Crean's father-in-law, Jack Harbaugh, asked Tom Zupancic, former strength coach and vice president of the Indianapolis Colts, to address the players before they went out for pre-game drills. One of the motivational props Zupancic used during his talk was a lunch pail. Crean also used the lunch pail to remind the team of the work ethic it had used all year to get to the tournament. Like the Superdome photo and baseball bat, this prop followed the team down the Road to the Final Four.

Marquette took the court during its scheduled 10:30 a.m. practice time for the Saturday matinee against the Big 12's Missouri Tigers. Crean had the Golden Eagles working on their match-up zone. There was a lot of yelling, with players letting each other know where they were supposed to be on the floor. This was how Crean's Crew was communicating and getting ready for the Tigers, who were four-and-a-half-point favorites.

As the starting lineups were being announced, the Marquette Band's "Ring Out Ahoya" could be heard over the din of the announced crowd of 25,767 at the RCA Dome. There were swatches of gold throughout the stadium. This would be the eighth meeting all-time between the schools, with Missouri holding a 4-3 series edge.

Crean felt that the game would be won in the trenches. The key matchup as far as he was concerned would be Missouri's 6'9" Arthur Johnson, the leading shot-blocker in Missouri history, and 6'10" Robert Jackson, who had scored just four points on two-of-seven shooting against Holy Cross. He and Merritt were a combined four of 17 in the Holy Cross game. That did not bode well against the load that Johnson was bringing.

"Tom Crean looks much more relaxed before this game than he did before the Holy Cross game," noted CBS announcers Gus Johnson and Len Elmore.

Marquette, wearing its white uniforms, opened with the match-up zone. Missouri Junior Rickey Paulding was determined to break that zone, as he started the game with a three-pointer. The Tigers opened with a man-to-man defense, which didn't seem to faze the Golden Eagles as they ran their first offensive sets.

Diener looked very confident running the smooth offense, and he did a nice job of crossing up the Tigers by driving to the basket when he saw an opening. Missouri was expecting him to camp outside in three-point-land for spot-up jumpers. Play-by-play man Gus Johnson favorably compared Diener to former Georgia Tech and Cleveland Cavalier guard Mark Price.

After a driving Diener lay-up, Elmore gushed, "That's a scrapper, right there. I'd play with that kid anytime."

At the 14:30 mark, Dan Rather cut in with his first report on "America At War," reporting on the large number of anti-war demonstrators marching in New York City. "When news breaks out, we'll break in," reminded Rather.

In addition to the confident play of Diener, Marquette was getting nice play off its bench. After Steve Novak came in for Todd Townsend, he hit his first three-pointer at the 12:15 mark of the first half. A nice start, since his three point shots were not falling at the Friday night shootaround.

Even during an NCAA Tournament game Crean continued to teach. When Townsend came out of the game, Crean demonstrated the proper defensive stance for his sophomore forward. Instead of yelling and scream-ing at his players, Crean instructed them on what they needed to improve, gave them a quick pat on the rear end, and sent them off. As loud and voluble as he can be when shouting instructions from the bench, he never embarrasses players in front of their teammates or the crowd. And it was not unusual for Crean to shout himself hoarse at a game or a practice.

Elmore noted that Marquette continued to confuse Missouri with its changing defenses. "It's a very aggressive zone. And I like the way they are finding people."

Moreover, Marquette was spacing the floor well in its possessions and getting back nicely in defensive transition. Merritt, who was just two of 10 in the Holy Cross game, was pushing Johnson farther and farther out of the lane, which limited the Tigers to just one shot each time down the floor. When Johnson was in deep, he had success underneath. But Mer-ritt consistently kept him away from the basket. As a result, Missouri began forcing up shots from long distance during the first half.

Junior Ricky Clemons tied the game at 20, just as CBS announcer Gus Johnson was saying that, "Snyder needs Clemons to hit a few." But it would be Clemons' only three-pointer of the game, as he went one of 10 from three-point range (two of 15 overall). Clemons was not a factor in the game.

After Diener stole the ball and made a lay-up, giving Marquette a 29-26 lead, Elmore exclaimed, "That guy is everywhere!"

With just over three and a half minutes left in the half, Missouri was shooting just 9 of 25 from the floor. "The Tigers are getting away from their inside-outside game," warned Elmore. Marquette was up 31-26, and shooting 57 percent from the field.

Marquette's bench erupted after another three-pointer, this one from another member of its fraternity, Joe Chapman, which drew a concerned look from Snyder. "Marquette is establishing both the inside and outside attacks," said Elmore.

While Wade had just six points with 2:14 remaining, he was finding his openings, not forcing the action, and letting the game come to him, as he had all season. "Wade came to play in the first half of this game, unlike the Holy Cross game," noted Johnson.

After the Golden Eagles upped their lead to 36-26, Snyder called a time-out, and it seemed like the Marquette Band played "Ring Out Ahoya" louder and louder each time it was highlighted during the game.

After the time-out, Clemons hit a two-point shot, and then Paulding hit a three to narrow the lead to 36-31.

Chapman then answered with a three of his own with 44 seconds left in the half, followed by a foul on Wade, whose free throws gave Marquette a 10-point margin, 41-31. Marquette's bench, which had been maligned late in the regular season, was now coming through big, with baskets from Novak, Chapman, and Karon Bradley—all freshmen.

CBS sideline reporter Solomon Wilcox asked Crean after the half how well he thought his match-up zone was working. "Well, I think it did. We want to do a good job defensively with our zone, and we want to attack a zone. We just work through this foul trouble a little bit and keep getting good shots, you know, I like our chances."

In the CBS "At The Half" show, while Clark Kellogg was impressed with Paulding's 14 points, he was more impressed with Wade's overall marks of eight points, three rebounds, four assists, and two steals. "That's what I call stuffing the stat sheet." He added that Marquette was judicious in its use of the three-point shot in the inside-outside game.

Before the start of the second half, a frustrated Snyder was interviewed and said, "We've gotta find a way to get the ball inside."

There was more of a sense of urgency to Missouri's game at the start of the second half. Paulding skied to slam home a missed shot, and Marquette turned the ball over in its first two possessions. Wade was then called for his second foul.

Marquette's lead was 41-33, but when Diener looked up and saw Wade streaking down the court, he hit him with a court-length pass that Wade converted for a lay-up. Elmore was impressed with the fact that Diener kept his head up and spotted Wade, "who was doing it all for Marquette."

And Paulding was doing it all for Mizzou. He was doing everything in his power to keep the Tigers in the game with his fourth and fifth three-pointers, narrowing the Marquette lead to eight (49-41). Mizzou was just starting to attack Marquette's defense.

"Missouri is starting to assert itself," noted Elmore, as the lead was cut to 51-45. Paulding was smoking with 22 points, while Wade had 12. Wade then hit a couple of jump shots to increase the lead to 55-44. "Wade has put together two good halves," Elmore noted, "and Missouri has forgotten what it took to cut into Marquette's lead."

Paulding then answered with another three. Marquette 55, Missouri 50. Another Missouri basket forced Crean to call a time-out at the 11:38 mark. "He's got that feel," Johnson said of Paulding, as "Ring Out Ahoya" rang out even louder in the RCA Dome.

The inside game was now starting to open up for Mizzou as a result of Paulding's torrid shooting. However, a Diener three upped Marquette's lead to 58-52. It was his first basket of the second half. The Golden Eagles then began to extend their zone defense.

Dan Rather interrupted the flow of the game with another cut-in at the 10:53 mark, as Marquette added a basket to go up 60-54. Paulding hurt his left (non-shooting) wrist, forcing him to leave the game. Diener then followed with another three. Marquette 64, Missouri 54. Marquette was getting very good ball movement both inside and outside.

After trading baskets, Marquette went up by 10 again, 66-56. At the 8:23 mark, Paulding returned with a taped-up left wrist. This was followed by another Diener three-pointer. Marquette 69-61.

Another Diener three at the 6:17 mark upped the lead to 74-67. The ever-confident Diener was "letting the game come to him," according to Johnson. "He's really lit it up," concurred Elmore.

Merritt joined the action, hitting his sixth field goal in seven attempts, putting the Golden Eagles up 76-68. "He's nifty with the ball," said Elmore.

As Diener brought the ball up with just over five minutes remaining and the Golden Eagles leading, 76-71, he looked over at Crean for the play, as the coach calmly kept his hands behind his back, pacing a little more slowly than he had earlier in the game.

A pair of Novak free throws put Marquette up 78-71. Two Paulding free throws made it 78-73, and Elmore opined that Missouri had "given up too quickly on getting Arthur Johnson back in the game."

Marquette then spread the floor with three minutes left and a three-point lead, 78-75. As Novak hustled to get a rebound, Elmore pointed out that "There was no effort by Missouri to go after loose balls."

As the fairly good-sized Marquette contingent could feel a victory coming on, chants of WE ARE MARQUETTE were beginning to reverberate strongly throughout the building.

At the 2:08 mark, Missouri called time-out after the Tigers' Travon Bryant fouled out. Bryant scored no points in the game and was not a factor. This brought Merritt to the line for a one-and-one, and a chance to extend Marquette's three-point lead and possibly put the game away.

The 78 percent free-throw shooter missed, and Paulding quickly answered with a game-tying three-pointer. Marquette 78, Missouri 78.

Marquette then called time-out.

Out of the time-out, Wade hit a jumper to put the Golden Eagles up 80-78. Missouri quickly called a time-out, with just over 30 seconds left in regulation.

Robert Jackson's foul on Arthur Johnson ended Jackson's day, but he was putting a 55-percent free-throw shooter on the line. Snyder was smiling for one of the few times all game. Johnson hit both free throws to tie the game at 80 apiece.

Diener brought the ball up with just over 19 seconds left. Wade missed a shot, and then Paulding missed a desperation shot, sending the game into overtime.

Crean went onto the court to greet the players, clapping his hands, encouraging them, just as he did that night at Freedom Hall at the end of February.

"Missouri has the momentum," Elmore stated. "Marquette has to just remember what got them to a 10-point lead."

Marquette controlled the overtime tip. Novak started out quickly by hitting a three-pointer. While the Golden Eagles were playing tough defense, Jimmy McKinney hit a three-pointer to tie the game at 83. Dan Rather then came on for his fourth "America at War" update at the 4:10 mark of the overtime.

Marquette was up 88-85 when Arthur Johnson was fouled. Once again, he made both free throws, narrowing the lead to 88-87. Mizzou went into a 2-3 zone, but Wade was able to sneak into the heart of the defense for a jumper, a result of Novak's zone-breaking accuracy. Marquette up 90-87.

After Missouri answered, Novak hit another three, increasing the lead to 93-89. "Novak scored over a seven-footer," exclaimed Elmore.

At the 1:45 mark, Diener was clapping his hands during a time-out as CBS went to a break with the "Holy Mackerel" call by the late Al McGuire, from the 1992 NCAA Tournament, his first for CBS, when Georgia Tech freshman James Forrest hit the first three-pointer of his season to defeat USC at the Bradley Center. "Only in college basketball," McGuire's voice trails at the end of the clip.

And only in college basketball could a freshman have the poise to take over an NCAA Tournament game—in overtime! Novak was a 52 percent three-point shooter during the season. Diener led Conference USA with a 44.2 percent mark his freshman year.

As the chants of WE ARE MARQUETTE grew louder, Diener, confident and poised as ever, found Merritt for an easy lay-up behind the defense. The lead was 95-89. After Diener was fouled and made both free throws, it was 97-89.

"It looks like they're gonna head to Minneapolis," Johnson said. "It was Missouri's inability to find Novak on the three-point line. Novak has ice water in his veins," said Elmore. Marquette went up by 10 points once again, 99-89, on two Wade free throws.

Marquette fans then began chanting WE WANT DIENER, WE WANT DIENER. The Marquette faithful were on their feet. Diener hit Marquette's last two points, followed by a Paulding three-pointer for the 101-92 final score. Crean and Snyder embraced and shook hands after a memorable game.

Marquette was perfect from the field in overtime (6 for 6) and at the free-throw line (6 for 6). Novak hit three three-pointers and four for the game. Marquette was an impressive 12 of 18 from three-point land. As a team, it shot 56.5 percent from the field and 66.7 percent from three-point range.

The Golden Eagles' balance was an important key. Diener led all Marquette scorers with 26 on eight of 12 shooting (5 of 8 three pointers), Wade had 24 points, eight rebounds, seven assists, two steals, and four turnovers. Merritt had a solid 18 points and Novak 14. But what was even more impressive was the bench, which was a perfect eight of eight from the field for 25 points.

Paulding (43 minutes) led all scorers with an incredible 36 points, on nine of 15 from three-point range. His partner Johnson (44 minutes) had a double-double with 28 points and 18 rebounds in a tough, losing cause. But Mizzou had no balance, as the rest of the team shot 4 of 27 from the field.

From his performance, it was apparent that Wade was just warming up. He let the game come to him, and when it came time to step up, he did. Diener was confident, and when he was not shooting or passing, he was looking to drive into the defense. He picked his spots beautifully, confusing the defenses thrown up against him.

Diener's performance earned him ESPN's "Player of the Day," and Marquette a Sweet 16 berth for the first time since 1994. This was also the first time that both Marquette and the University of Wisconsin had advanced to the Sweet 16 in the same NCAA Tournament. Wisconsin earned its berth with a narrow win over Tulsa following Marquette's victory.

"When Marquette beat Missouri in overtime, we headed over to the team hotel in Indianapolis. There were 500 to 1,000 fans," recalled Jim Ganzer. "It was amazing. It was an impromptu pep rally.

"I was standing next to Bill Cords, who was talking to Crean on a cell phone, trying to get the team to return to the hotel. 'Spread the word. They're comin' back,'" Cords told the people around us. When they came back, Crean talked to the crowd, but it was so loud, no one could hear him, so they gave him a bullhorn. Then he brought out each of the players, class by class. They did it more formally in Minneapolis, though," Ganzer explained.

In the *Chicago Sun-Times'* preview of the Marquette-Pittsburgh game, a full color shot of Diener took up the entire back sports page below the headline "Oh, Baby!" The subhead read: "Travis Diener might look like he's still in high school, but the sophomore point guard has come of age for Marquette." And Brian Hanley's full-page profile of Diener appeared under the headline: "A Get-Tough Policy," in which Tom Crean is quoted as referring to his young guard as "tough, unselfish, and fearless."

Next stop: Minneapolis, where No. 3 seed Marquette (25-5) would face No. 2 seed Pittsburgh (28-4), the Big East champion, while Wisconsin would take on No. 1 Kentucky at the Hubert H. Humphrey Metrodome, Thursday evening, March 27. And both Wisconsin teams were ready for prime time.

Before the teams headed to Minneapolis, they returned home for a couple of days. At Marquette's Golden Eagle Gift Shop, Sweet 16 T-shirts and caps were being sold so quickly it was tough to keep them in stock. The lines outside the shop were extended outside the Alumni Memorial Union. When Crean, who turned 37 on Tuesday of that week, heard about how long people were waiting in line to buy the paraphernalia, he showed up and signed autographs. He signed caps, T-shirts, posters, pennants—you name it. The good feelings between the coach and the students, with whom he had bonded since he arrived, were obviously genuine.

A mass exodus of fans from both schools left Wisconsin for Minnesota. Unfortunately, with all of the good feeling there was tragedy. Best friends Lori Rosenblum and Amanda Schepers, both 24, and another motorist were killed in a four-car accident in St. Croix County, Wisconsin, on their way to Minneapolis for the Sweet 16. After she was graduated from Marquette in 2001, Rosenblum had driven to Milwaukee to see as many Marquette games as possible. Both were great Marquette basketball fans. Their deaths brought some perspective to all the excitement that was taking place in and around the team and school. Schepers was to graduate from Marquette in May.

When Thursday evening arrived, there was a huge contingent of Wisconsin and Marquette fans inside the Metrodome, an unusual color combo of red and gold among the crowd of 28,168. There was not a whole lot of Kentucky blue throughout the arena. "Kentucky fans just didn't bother to show up," noted John Baker, who added that, "They figured they were going to New Orleans."

In the first game, Wisconsin was a heavy underdog to top-ranked Kentucky, which carried a 25-game winning streak into the Sweet 16. But Wisconsin gamely hung tough throughout the first half and well into the second half, working the shot clock on its possessions.

With just over three minutes left in the first half, Kentucky's scoring leader, senior Keith Bogans, suffered a high ankle sprain and left the game. The Badgers were down by just four at the half. Bogans did not return for the second half, but the Badgers did not have any player who could stop the Marquis Estill freight train. The 6'9" senior Estill had 28 points and seemed to get his points every which way against Wisconsin.

Mike Wilkinson and Devin Harris helped reduce Kentucky's lead to three with under a minute left. Marquette and Wisconsin fans stood up and cheered in unison, LET'S GO RED! LET'S GO RED!

An uncharacteristic turnover and two missed free throws by Wilkinson, and Wisconsin was done. Losing to Kentucky by five, 63-57. Kentucky's winning streak was now 26. But the Badgers made the Wildcats look vulnerable. And beatable.

MARQUETTE 77, PITTSBURGH 74

In the evening's second game, Marquette would be facing a team that, like Holy Cross, came into the tournament on a nice winning streak (11 games). Pitt was holding teams to 38.6 percent shooting from the field and 30.3 percent from three-point range. The Panthers' defense manhandled Indiana, 74-52. But the one negative statistic was that the Panthers were shooting only 63.5 percent from the free-throw line. It was the fourth time in history that Marquette would play Pitt. The teams met in 1930, then again in 1974 and '75, with the Panthers holding a 2-1 series edge.

Crean and Pitt coach Ben Howland were both in their fourth year as head coaches, and had turned around their respective programs.

Howland, a southern California native, had attempted to fend off questions all during the week about whether he was going to replace Steve Lavin, who had been fired by UCLA after the Pac 10 Tournament. He was quoted as saying that the UCLA position was a "dream job," and that he had been a fan of the Bruins growing up in California. Howland had also indicated interest in the job.

The media looked at such statements as distracting to the team as it was preparing for its second straight Sweet 16 appearance. Winning the

Big East, its No. 2 seeding, and the way Pitt took care of Indiana earlier in the week made the Panthers a six-point favorite over Marquette.

In the CBS pre-game segment with Clark Kellogg and Quin Snyder, both analysts picked Marquette to prevail, based on the team's tough, changing defenses and the talent of Dwyane Wade. "Wade is analogous to a dolly," noted Kellogg, "he does all the heavy lifting."

When the conversation turned to Bogans, Kellogg noted that "In the short term, Kentucky could pull together and hope that Bogans can get healthy for New Orleans."

As CBS went to commercial, the confident and smiling faces of the Marquette Band filled the camera, as Al McGuire's "Holy Mackerel" call was aired before the game.

Marquette wore its blue uniforms, while its large contingent of fans were dressed in gold filling up the Metrodome. The Golden Eagles had a rather inauspicious beginning, missing five of their first six shots, as Pittsburgh extended a 5-2 margin to 8-2 on a Donatas Zavackas' three-pointer. The senior from Lithuania was the Panthers' best three-point shooter, at just over 44 percent. "He's been known to have confrontations with his teammates and Howland from time to time," noted game analyst Raftery, who covered the Big East for ESPN during the regular season.

Pitt extended its lead to 15-8 after Diener missed his first two three-pointers. Crean began substituting early, bringing in Novak and Chapman. At the 11:50 mark, Marquette had four turnovers and just three field goals. "What happened to Novak and Diener?" asked an exasperated Raftery, who broadcast the game with veteran CBS play-by-play man Verne Lundquist.

Zavackas and Wade both had two fouls by the 10-minute mark of the first half. And it was Marquette's big players—Merritt and Jackson—who were doing the heavy lifting. On one move by Merritt, where he finished off the glass, Raftery was complimentary of the progress the junior had made during the course of the season.

"Off-season work, preseason individual drills. His skill level, I think, is extraordinary. Here he is, able to gather himself, and use that window with such an affectionate mannerism," said Raftery, giving his best Jackie Gleason imitation. Lundquist's response: "And awaaaay we go!"

Marquette took its first lead of the game (22-21) since it led 2-0 at the game's start, on a Todd Townsend three-pointer off a Wade feed. With four minutes left, Pitt retook the lead, 23-22.

Diener, who was still bothered by shin splints, hit for two over Julius Page, and then set up Novak with a three to put Marquette ahead 27-25. Page then answered with his own three-pointer. Pittsburgh went up 28-27, which spurred Lundquist to remark: "This one has lived up to expectations."

The rest of the half went back and forth, as the teams traded baskets and free throws. The teams were well matched and played tough defense.

As Raftery and Lundquist watched Crean pick up his pace on the sidelines, Lundquist remarked, "I think he's gonna age another six years before this game is over." "The job he's done with this program, all the Jesuits are praying for him. They give him the collection," joked Raftery, who was the special guest at Crean's first Midnight Madness four years earlier and had watched the team grow. He also mentioned good news for Trey Schwab, that Crean's special assistant had moved to the top of the lung donor list. Leslie Visser mentioned that Schwab wore a vibrating device that alerted him when a donor would become available.

As Pitt Coach Howland was interviewed at the end of the half, with the game tied at 34, he commented, "These are both very good teams. It's been a back-and-forth game. We've been hurt in transition. We've gotta stay at home with the shooters. We've been hurt in transition. They've hit some difficult shots."

While Wade scored only two points in the half on one of five shooting, and Diener was just one of four, Marquette as a team was shooting 46 percent and 5 of 10 from three-point range, while the Panthers were at 47 percent and three of seven from beyond the arc. Pittsburgh had 17 rebounds, Marquette 14, and the teams were very even in assists, with Pitt getting 10 and Marquette 9.

Before the second half resumed, Dan Rather cut in for an "America at War" update, describing the "most severe night of bombings in Baghdad yet."

Robert Jackson put Marquette ahead with two free throws early in the second half, and as the Golden Eagles returned on defense, they slapped the floor, waiting for the Panthers.

A Brandin Knight three put Pitt ahead, 37-36. But just three minutes into the second half, Wade began to take charge. A Wade lay-in gave the Golden Eagles a 39-37 lead. Wade then fed Jackson for a lay-up, upping the lead to 41-37, Marquette's largest lead of the game up to that point.

"Jackson is having a ball underneath the rim," noted Raftery. "All of a sudden, the tempo favors Marquette, the aggressive play favors Marquette."

The Marquette students were on their feet chanting, WE ARE MAR-QUETTE, as Wade hit a jumper that extended the lead to 43-37. Lundquist then asked, "Could this be the game where free-throw deficiency catches up with Pittsburgh?"

Wade exploded for 10 straight points. And he was just starting to heat up, Raftery warned, "School's out unless they get control of Wade." But as Pitt continued to keep the game within five points, Raftery added, "Pitt is comfortable in close encounters."

After a Novak three-pointer put Marquette up by seven, Raftery described the much smaller Knight on Novak as a "nightmare match-up."

Then came one of the great plays of the tournament. As Wade made his approach to the paint, his arm was pulled by Jaron Brown yet he still managed to move toward the basket, was hit by Ontario Lett (described by Raftery as a "municipal sanitary landfill"), fell, and just threw the ball up to the basket, where it went in. It was Jordanesque.

"Amazing use of the dribble. The automatic switch on the perimeter. This deft ability. Here's the switch, to Brown. Now watch this one, Verne. In between the show guy, the slide by, the pull down, the strength to get it up there. And the joy and satisfaction. Oh, what a job well done. And this is utterly incredible." And Wade completed the three-point play. When Wade's shot went in, that was when viewers in Marquette Nation knew it was their night.

"There are some maneuvers for which there is no defense," added Lundquist.

"And it's Pittsburgh's fault for letting him get in the game. He's [Wade] struggling, he got loose, and they feed off him, this Marquette team. They gotta close him down. Mainly in the box area," warned Raftery.

"You'll never see that shot again in college basketball," Diener told Bill Livingston of the *Cleveland Plain Dealer*. Livingston added: "You've barely seen that shot from Kobe Bryant, Michael Jordan, or Dr. J."

As Marquette continued to hold on to a six-point lead, one of the strangest events to take place in an NCAA Tournament game unfolded on the Pittsburgh bench. Zavackas, for one reason or another, refused to join his team in its previous four huddles. He sat on the floor, away from the bench, and took off his shoes.

CBS sideline reporter Leslie Visser asked the team doctor what brought it on. He said, "You'll have to ask Howland."

Lundquist noted a "glum-looking" Pittsburgh bench. At the 5:30 mark, Zavackas was still sitting on the floor, as Marquette's lead was extended to 70-59 on an emphatic Wade dunk. "It's the D, it's the spirit, it's the emotion. Send it in!" Raftery gushed, clearly enjoying the exhibition Wade was putting on.

After a Marquette time-out, the Golden Eagles slowed it down and began to milk the clock. Marquette's sweat started to dry and Pitt went on an 11-1 run to cut the lead to 71-70.

During that run, the Golden Eagles did not seem to get flustered by Pitt's forays into the paint for easy lay-ups. It was not until the 2:12 mark that Zavackas finally rejoined his team on the bench.

The Marquette bench locked its arms for the last 1:17 of regulation. After a Knight lay-in narrowed the margin to 73-72, Wade made another outstanding drive to the hoop, complete with jump stop and, as Raftery described it, "the kiss." "That could go down in Marquette memory."

Knight was fouled on a lay-up, making it a 75-74 game. Merritt was fouled bringing the ball up-court. He "doesn't hit the rim" with his free throws, said Raftery. Marquette up 77-74, with just over 11 seconds.

Knight then pulled the trigger on a three-pointer too quickly, and Diener got the rebound and was fouled. "This is a tough-minded group, this Marquette team," admired Raftery. Diener uncharacteristically missed both free throws and Pitt tried a desperation three that missed.

Marquette won, 77-74, as the Golden Eagle fans and students stormed the court at the Metrodome, celebrating Marquette's entrance into the NCAA's Elite Eight. Also, Marquette ended Pitt's 11-game winning streak, and Pitt became the fourth conference champion to be defeated by the Golden Eagles during the season.

Wade scored 20 of his 22 points in the second half, followed by Merritt's 17, Jackson's 16, Novak's nine, Bradley's six and, most surprising of all, Diener's four. After scoring 55 points in his first two games, he was nearly shut down. Even though he was still bothered by shin splints, Diener did not turn the ball over once. In three games—Holy Cross, Missouri, and Pitt—Diener had one turnover!

"After the Pittsburgh game, there were long lines of fans hoping to meet the players at the Crowne Plaza Hotel in Minneapolis," recalled photographer John Baker. "When the players showed up at the hotel, the fans all wanted autographs. Travis was posing for pictures and giving autographs. He was like the mayor.

"You could see some of the players wanting to go home. It was 1 a.m. They have to play their biggest game of the year in 30 hours and here they are signing autographs," continued Baker, who was impressed with the players' patience.

The *Chicago Sun-Times* sports page was filled with a large color shot of Joe Chapman signaling "No. 1" above the headline, "Regal Eagles." The *Chicago Tribune's* top sports headline the next day read: "Marquette Up To Task," with a smiling color photo of Steve Novak looking out at readers.

Chicago Tribune columnist Rick Morrissey predicted in his column the next day that Kentucky could be beaten. "It might take an aligning of the planets, an injury or two, and the continued absence of Kentucky superfan Ashley Judd, but it can happen.

"Or maybe all it will take is the continued presence of Marquette superman Dwyane Wade."

When Kentucky played Wisconsin, former Crean assistant (now UW–Green Bay coach) Tod Kowalczyk came back to help his old boss prep for the Sweet 16. Kowalczyk watched films of Wisconsin and was at the game to scout the Badgers.

After Kentucky prevailed, Kowalczyk reportedly told Crean that Kentucky was beatable. Crean assistant Darrin Horn was in charge of preparing the game plan for the Kentucky game.

"After the [Kentucky-Wisconsin] game, all of the people were taking off their red shirts to reveal Marquette gold T-shirts," recalled Baker. "There were more Marquette fans than Pittsburgh fans. Much louder, too."

In the team's Friday practice in preparation for Kentucky, Crean stated that it was the best that he had ever seen Wade in practice.

MARQUETTE 83, KENTUCKY 69

The March 29 game between Marquette and Kentucky was 26 years and one day after McGuire's Warriors won the 1977 national championship. Kentucky's 26-game winning streak was on the line and the Wildcats were without the full services of their leading scorer, Keith Bogans, hobbled with the high ankle sprain he had suffered in the Wisconsin game.

In the time leading up to the game, the media began asking questions of players on both teams. Kentucky center Marquis Estill was asked if he remembered having played against Marquette's Robert Jackson when the 6'10" center was playing for Mississippi State. Estill honestly answered that he did not remember playing against him and did not know that he was at Mississippi State. He also stated that if Marquette tried to play him with one man, it would be a long day. That was all the bulletin board material that Jackson and Marquette needed.

Leslie Visser told Verne Lundquist that the Midwest Regional Final was "Marquis versus Marquette in a Marquee Match-up."

The night before the game, Crean received a "good-luck" phone call from Oklahoma coach Kelvin Sampson, with whom Crean had worked on Jud Heathcote's staff at Michigan State back in 1989. In the locker room before the game, Crean relied on his motivational tactics once again, by showing his players the caps of the previous seven college and professional sports champions (excluding the Los Angeles Lakers), and telling them stories of how each of those teams were not supposed to win their respective sports' championship, but did. All were underdogs, just like Marquette.

This would be the ninth NCAA game between the teams, each having won four of the previous matches. As a result of this tournament history, and the other games over the years, there really was no intimidation factor working against Marquette. As Kentucky marked its basketball centennial, it had not dominated Marquette in NCAA Tournament play as it had other teams.

The first meeting between the teams was back in 1955, when Jack Nagle's 24-3 Warriors went up against Rupp's #2 ranked Wildcats in the second round in Evanston, Illinois. Nagle defeated the Baron of the Bluegrass, 79-71, to advance to the third round where Marquette lost to Iowa 86-81.

In 1959, Eddie Hickey's Warriors lost to Rupp's #2 Wildcats 98-69, in a Mideast Regional consolation game, also in Evanston.

Nine years later, Rupp was still coaching in Lexington when he faced Al McGuire in a Mideast Regional Semifinal in Lexington—hardly a neutral court. It was the first time the coaches had met in a game. After some verbal histrionics between the two because McGuire insisted on being paid before going on Rupp's television show, the Warriors were blown out by the Wildcats 107-89.

The next year the tables were turned as Marquette played Kentucky in the old Field House in Madison, Wisconsin. Led by a courageous George Thompson, the Warriors prevailed in the Mideast Regional Semifinal, 81-74, before losing in the regional final to Rick Mount and Purdue. The Boilermakers would go on to lose to UCLA in the 1969 NCAA Finals.

McGuire defeated Rupp again two years later, but this time it was in a Mideast Regional consolation game, 91-74, in Athens, Georgia.

The last game McGuire coached against Rupp was in the 1972 NCAA, in which the Warriors lost a Mideast Regional Semifinal to the Wildcats 85-69, in Dayton, OH, at the Mideast Region. It was Rupp's last win as a coach.

Three years later, in another Mideast Regional Semifinal, this one in Tuscaloosa, Alabama, Marquette lost to Joe B. Hall's Wildcats, 76-54.

Marquette would not play Kentucky again in the NCAA Tournament until 1994, when Kevin O'Neill's Warriors tangled with Rick Pitino's Wildcats. A tough defensive game, featuring the great guard play of Tony Miller, helped lead Marquette to a 75-63 win, in St. Petersburg, Florida, vaulting the Warriors into the Sweet 16, where they lost to Duke.

The headline of Brian Hanley's preview of the game in the *Chicago Sun-Times* read: "They Play Like Warriors."

And Crean would face Tubby Smith, who told CBS before the game that this was "the most talented team that I've had."

In the studio before the game, Clark Kellogg said that while Wade was superb, "Chuck Hayes can match up with Wade," but "Kentucky is going to have to probe inside and take more perimeter shots than they are comfortable taking."

Quin Snyder felt that Kentucky would win because their "defense can force turnovers and get points off turnovers."

"This Marquette team may be as special as that '77 team was," noted studio host Greg Gumbel. Added Kellogg, "I think they can overcome Kentucky because they have more offense." When speaking of Wade, Kellogg reminded Gumbel and Snyder, "He's a dolly, he can carry the heavy load."

CBS framed the matchup as "David versus Goliath," with Marquette going up against the powerful Goliath that was Kentucky. With seven national championships and a 26-game winning streak, the Wildcats were a six-and-a-half-point favorite.

Lundquist and Raftery were once again behind the mikes for this Midwest Regional Final. They opened the broadcast with information regarding Bogans, who had not really tested his ankle in warm-ups, according to sideline reporter Leslie Visser, but still gave her the thumbs-up sign "that he was ready to go."

After talking about Wade, CBS played a tape where Wade basically introduced himself on the staircase of the Old Gym. "The strength of my game is, I'm all heart. Our goal is to get to New Orleans and no one is gonna get in our way," as he stared straight into the intruding camera without blinking or flinching. And you believed him.

Raftery's keys to the game included the importance of Marquette's transition defense and a warning that Kentucky could not let Wade "get off."

Things did not start well for Marquette as Wade turned it over on the team's first possession. Kentucky was applying its man-to-man pressure, and began getting easy lay-ups and baseline drives. "That is dangerous for Marquette," warned Raftery. "Marquette is not doing a lot of good things defensively. There's no help on the baseline drives, no help in the box."

Watching Bogans on the floor, especially on defense, Raftery and Lundquist both agreed that he was "very restricted" in his movements.

Marquette looked disorganized and was slow getting back on defense. Kentucky was not running away with the game, but was threatening a quick knockout blow before Marquette could get untracked. Nothing was coming easy for the Golden Eagles.

At the 15:29 mark, Lundquist said, going to commercial, "8-7, Golden Warriors."

The game seemed to go back and forth for the first 10 minutes, with the teams exchanging leads almost every possession. Wade's first points of the game came at the 13:13 mark of the half when he showed some "serious hops" on a slam dunk, according to Raftery, and hung on the rim just a little longer for effect—as if to let the Wildcats know of things to come. Marquette was up 10-9.

At the 11:34 mark, Wade hit a jumper, narrowing the Kentucky lead to 14-13. Wade then hit Jackson for a lay-in. "Just a blow-by," said Raftery of the way that Wade set up Jackson. "It's all Wade."

Wade then set up Karon Bradley for a three. As a number of Kentucky "white shirts" converged on Wade, he dished off to an open Bradley. Marquette 18-14.

Marquette now was starting to turn the tables on Kentucky by turning up the defensive pressure, forcing the Wildcats into taking low-percentage shots as the shot clock wound down.

Each team traded baskets over about a two-minute period, which was climaxed by another Wade "NCAA moment." Wade blocked a shot by Marquis Estill, then took off down the court and put up a reverse lay-up that was goal-tended by Kentucky. Marquette 26-19.

"Just keep playin'," urged a clearly ecstatic Raftery. "Let me enjoy this, Verne. I mean, his changes of speeds and body control as he blows by guys. And then the understanding of traffic and responsibility. You put it up, they're gonna block it, and there's a fast break the other way. But dipsy-do, my goodness!"

Lundquist reminded Raftery that Wade was not a McDonald's All-American. "He went to McDonald's, he was not a McDonald's All-American," Raftery laughed.

At the 5:24 mark, MU was up by 29-19. In the previous 7:25, Kentucky had scored only one field goal. "Kentucky is not efficient at the offensive end. Marquette has taken that away," Raftery pointed out.

Travis Diener's three-pointer at the 4:54 mark put Marquette up, 32-19, in the midst of a 22-5 run. After a Novak miss, Merritt slammed it home as the Marquette students and fans, almost an all-gold Metrodome, stood up and cheered.

Marquette increased the lead to 35-21 on a three-pointer from Novak, with an assist to Wade. Fourteen points was the largest deficit Kentucky had faced all season. Novak followed with another three-pointer, this time from Diener.

The lead ballooned to 40-24 with two minutes remaining. Novak hit another three to make it 43-24. Another Wade assist for a Jackson basket, and Marquette was up 45-24. Kentucky, down by 21 points? It was inconceivable.

With 18.8 seconds remaining in the first half, Tubby Smith called time-out, as WE ARE MARQUETTE reverberated throughout the Metrodome. Kentucky did score before the half ended, making it 45-26. And as Lundquist said, "It was an amazing first half," with Marquette going on a 27-11 run in the last eight minutes.

"I think the dish ran away with the spoon," stated Leslie Visser to Crean as he was coming off the floor. "Well, you know we're moving the ball on offense, we're attacking the rim a little bit and getting driving kick shots, and defensively we started blocking out better after the first five minutes," remarked Crean. Visser then asked, "Will you tell your team they are 20 minutes away from the Final Four?" "I'll tell them it's 0-0," smiled Crean.

As the camera focused on the Kentucky band after the interview, some of the band members were gamely saying, "There's a whole other half left."

In the CBS Studio, Greg Gumbel noted that, "There's a clinic going on in Minneapolis, and it's not being conducted by Kentucky, but by Dwyane Wade and the Marquette Warriors."

Wade scored 11 points, had eight rebounds, seven assists, and four blocks. "He's a stat-sheet stuffer supreme," Kellogg said of Wade. When they showed his block of the shot and drive that was goal-tended, Kellogg described it as "bagging your own groceries."

Snyder felt that Kentucky could get back in the game if it took the comeback in four-minute segments.

Dan Rather's cut-in during halftime focused on bombs continuing to fall on Baghdad, suicide bombers, and Iraqi officials promising "to follow the enemy into its own land."

Early in the second half, there was a scary moment for Wade as he ran into another player on the baseline. Wade went down and held his knee, and you could hear every Marquette fan throughout the country gasp.

As it turned out, he banged kneecaps with a Wildcat. After wincing and walking, Wade seemed to be OK.

Wade, Diener, Jackson, and Novak helped Marquette maintain at least a 12-point lead through the first 10 minutes of the second half. At the 11:38 mark CBS played the "Holy Mackerel" clip as Marquette fans were chanting louder and louder, WE ARE MARQUETTE. WE ARE MARQUETTE. WE ARE MARQUETTE.

The lead was 59-47, with just under 10 minutes to play, when Steve Novak, quick on his feet in the paint, stepped in to take a charge. That could very well have been a turning point in the game, had the call gone the other way. The basket would have counted and a free throw would have cut Marquette's lead to nine. As it turned out, the quick-thinking freshman was in the right place at the right time.

A Merritt runner from Wade made it 61-47, Marquette, and the chant started up again. WE ARE MARQUETTE. WE ARE MARQUETTE.

Wade made an exclamation jam over Estill, upping Marquette's margin to 64-47. His three-point basket made it 67-49, which prompted this Raftery gem: "A little bit like honey. PURE!" Another Wade dunk made it 69-52. And then another. Marquette up 71-54. "He is just going anywhere he wants," said Raftery, as Wade scored 11 straight points for the Golden Eagles. And then another dunk, increasing the lead to 76-57.

"I hope he likes Cajun food," noted Lundquist. "Jambalaya!" gushed Raftery. "They're 4:44 away," added Lundquist.

By the 4:02 mark, Wade had a triple double. Only two other players in NCAA history had accomplished that feat: Utah's Andre Miller in 1998 and Earvin "Magic" Johnson of Michigan State in 1979.

When speaking of Diener, Raftery said, "He does look angelic, but he would steal your hubcaps. He has a little larceny in his heart."

At the 3:38 mark, Marquette led 77-59, and as the team was getting back on defense, Wade was slapping the floor. He was not done yet. The lead went back to 20, when Wade fed Jackson. Marquette 79, Kentucky 59.

With just over a minute and a half left, the *piece de resistance* was a Diener pass to Novak, and before Novak even caught the pass Diener turned toward the other end of the floor and raised his arms in the air signaling a three-point basket. And Novak's shot was good. And he was fouled. "As good as I've seen in recent memory," Raftery noted.

The Marquette-heavy crowd erupted with WE ARE MARQUETTE. WE ARE MARQUETTE. WE ARE MARQUETTE. As the fans and students held up copies of the *Marquette Tribune's* special edition with the headline, HOLY MACKEREL!

As the CBS cameras panned the Kentucky bench, the faces of the Wildcats were flushed with shock. Their last loss was Dec. 28 at Louisville. A 26-game winning streak, the longest in the country. Ended. Bogans, who never missed a game as a collegian, played gamely on a gimpy ankle and scored 15 points in his final game as a senior.

On the other bench, Diener hugged Crean as he came off the floor. Crean then sent walk-on Jared Sichting, son of former Boston Celtics' player Jerry Sichting, into the game.

As the game wound down, Steve "The Homer" True and George Thompson were enjoying every last second, as Marquette was salting the game away. Right toward the end, Thompson backed away from the microphone to compose himself. It was an emotional and memorable ending for Thompson, whose connection to the Marquette-Kentucky series goes back to the McGuire era.

Wade's numbers: 29 points, 11 rebounds, and 11 assists. He was starting to become known as "Mr. 29-11-11." Most Outstanding Player of the Midwest Regional. And Chuck Hayes, the man who guarded Wade: 0 points, five fouls.

Marquette fans could not storm the court after this win, because security was ready for them, unlike after the Pittsburgh game.

Apart from defeating another conference champion (Kentucky went undefeated during the SEC season), it was the first time ever in the storied history of Marquette basketball that it had beaten a team ranked number one in the country. That never happened during the McGuire Era.

When Thompson interviewed Wade after the game, he told the All-America that he was the best basketball player to ever play for Marquette University. High praise indeed for the man who still holds the all-time record for points scored in a career. What George Thompson did for Al McGuire, Dwyane Wade was doing for Tom Crean. Later, Thompson gave a big bear hug to Robert Jackson, congratulating him on his performance against the Wildcats. Thompson was showing how incredibly proud he was of the only senior on the team in his only season at Marquette.

Marquette was the first team in the 2003 tournament to advance to the Final Four.

As Visser interviewed Crean and the players after the game, Wade proudly let everyone know that the victory was for all the Golden Eagles. And that the players believed in themselves. "We came out as a team. We've been working hard to get here."

A tired but happy Crean exclaimed, "This team will join the 1977 team as one of the best in Marquette history." Then Visser held up the Holy Mackerel! special edition upside down. CBS then went to the Holy Mackerel! Clip, which served as a very appropriate segue.

Only in college basketball. Can a team win every game but one as an underdog and get to the Final Four, and not be considered a Cinderella?

In Milwaukee, "the students who were watching the game at the Annex were asking each other, 'Are you running to the lake?'" noted Marquette senior Jaci Pabst, whose parents met at Marquette in 1977 and partied the night of the national championship. Her grandfather also went up to Milwaukee that night, and was buying rounds of drinks at Jim Hegarty's. After the '77 team won the title, Hegarty told him that all he had to pay for was the first drink he bought that night, and no more.

"We ran out of the Annex," Pabst continued. "And we were dancing in the middle of the street at 16th and Wells. There were helicopters circling above us. At the Campus Town student residence, students opened their windows, put their speakers in the windows, and were playing the Marquette Fight Song.

"We all got the same thought at once. We turned around and started running at once. From 16th and Wells, we ran down Wells to Schroeder Field, cut across the field to the parking lot behind the 1212 Building, to 12th and Wisconsin, and then down to the lake."

"We were marching, walking, and running," continued Pabst. "We were hugging each other. Guys were lifting girls on their shoulders. We chanted WE ARE MARQUETTE. The police had shut off the streets. People were cheering us on as we ran. Businesses along Wisconsin Avenue cheered us on. As far ahead as I could see, there were people. As far back as I could see, there were people."

They all went down to the lake, just like the kids had done 26 years before. All the way down to Lake Michigan. A few thousand headed down there. Other kids were hanging off lampposts, truly experiencing for the first time the feeling they had been hearing about for years, about that 1977 championship celebration.

"That's all I heard growing up. We'd better get to the championship. I called my parents and said, 'Now I know what you went through in 1977.'"

"For years, everyone talked about 1977," said Raymonds. "Now, all of a sudden, they're experiencing this for the first time. Now they know what it was all about in '77."

"Somewhere, Al McGuire is smiling," noted Greg Gumbel, who pointed out that the game was not Kentucky's worst NCAA Tournament loss. The Wildcats lost to Western Kentucky in 1971 by 24 points, and I don't think Dwyane Wade had anything to do with that."

As Crean and the team were cutting down the nets at the Metrodome, Crean motioned Marquette President Father Wild down to the court to cut down a strand. Said a delighted Father Wild, "I did not expect that, because I wanted them to have their moment. After all, they played. But he insisted."

"After our victory over Kentucky, I was standing, getting ready to give a talk, when I was asked if I could slide this phrase into my remarks— 'Final Four Million.' And it caught fire," noted Rev. Wild. "The phrase emanated from Julie Tolan, Al Frisone, and Ben Tracy. Within a week after the Final Four, we had surpassed our goal [of $31 million for the McGuire Center]. And there was no gift over six figures."

"The excitement and energy were just remarkable. When you reach the Final Four, that is rarefied air. We always know what we are building for," concluded the very proud Marquette president, who added that the university should see a big increase in admissions in the next year.

One of the great Kodak moments during the net-cutting was of Crean and his son, Riley, who was born not long after Crean was hired at Marquette, up there on the ladder, draped in nylon. One look at the photo and you can feel Crean's pride, especially with having his son join him at the basket.

As the basketball team and university began to get coast-to-coast coverage from newspapers and radio and TV outlets, pledges for the McGuire Center continued to grow. Columnists and writers and broadcasters were taking their Al McGuire stories out of the closet and dusting them off for a new generation of people who may never have heard of McGuire, except for this team's Final Four run. Monday's headline over Brian Hanley's story in the *Chicago Sun-Times* said it all: "CREAN'S EAGLES ARE REALLY FLYING HIGH."

What with everything happening in Iraq, and the bad news on other college basketball teams around the country, Marquette was a refreshing story in college sports. A team with a sharp, young coach, players who conducted themselves well, on and off the court, in and out of the classroom. And, of course, the Trey Schwab story also contributed to the "feel good" nature of the Marquette Madness. In fact, Marquette was one of only five schools in the Sweet 16 to graduate at least two-thirds of their players. The others: Butler, Duke, Notre Dame, and Kansas. Even casual basketball fans began pulling for Marquette. Headline writers were having a lot of fun with all of the "Marq Madness" going on all around the country.

Before the NCAA Tournament began, Marquette was still several million shy of the $31 million it needed to finish the McGuire Center and have enough for an operating endowment. Making the Final Four for the first time in 26 years was certainly a big boost to push fundraising over the top and have a surplus for the operating endowment.

Marquette was just beginning to learn what a Final Four berth in the NCAA Tournament was worth, in terms of positive national exposure, publicity, and a higher national profile: It was PRICELESS. ∎

CHAPTER FIVE:
DANCIN' ON
BOURBON STREET

During his broadcast career, whenever the NCAA Final Four was going to be held in New Orleans (1982, 1987, 1993), Al McGuire would tell schools whose games he was broadcasting that if they played well, "They could be dancin' on Bourbon Street."

The Marquette team was welcomed home on campus as conquering heroes late Saturday night, March 29. The tired, happy faces alighting from the bus were champions for another weekend. While they were enjoying their moment of glory, they also knew they had unfinished business ahead of them. A Final Four date with the Kansas Jayhawks was next. Coach Crean gave them a much deserved day off.

Crean, who slept little more than an hour the nights before tournament games, would be up early Sunday morning, March 30, watching film of the Jayhawks. That date happened to be the fourth anniversary of the signing of Crean's first contract at Marquette, and here he was taking his team to the Final Four. Heady stuff, indeed.

At St. James Church that morning, in Mequon, Wisconsin, where Father Tom DeVries was celebrating the service, he congratulated Crean and the team for a job well done and wished them well in New Orleans.

Crean was soon back at home, watching as much tape of Kansas as possible to prepare his team and getting prepared for a quick television visit in his home from Greg Gumbel and CBS for the network's pregame show that day. While Crean and his staff busied themselves, the students and fans were figuring out ways to get a flight to the Big Easy as well as a hotel. Crean even called Kansas coach Roy Williams to find out when the Jayhawks were heading to New Orleans and what their schedule entailed, such was the respectful relationship of the competing coaches.

Wednesday of that week came quickly, as the team was getting ready to leave Milwaukee for New Orleans. The team assembled outside the Union to say goodbye to the students and fans. When it was Wade's turn to talk, he told the students that the Golden Eagles were going to bring home a national championship, and the students erupted in cheers. Just what they wanted to hear from their superstar. When Crean talked, he did not promise a championship, but promised that the team would give its best effort.

That week there was concern because Wade's picture was on one of the regional covers of the April 7 issue of *Sports Illustrated*, 26 years after Butch Lee appeared on the April 4, 1977, "Marquette Makes Its Mark" issue after winning the national championship. Of course, the worries were about the *SI* Cover Jinx. But there were so many good feelings floating around, people did not pay that much attention to it.

A comparison between the 1977 and 2003 teams is instructive. While it is hard to compare players from different eras, there are always similarities and differences.

"You really can't compare," said Hank Raymonds. "We didn't have a shot clock and the three-point shot. I don't think Al would have been able to coach this team because of a lack of control. He wouldn't have had control."

Added John Fedders, "Al did not permit free-lancing on the basketball court during a game. The kind of freedom that Diener and Wade enjoyed would not have been permitted under Al McGuire."

"Most teams play today at a faster pace, and it has to do with the rules. We had better overall talent. It's hard to compare players from different eras," added Raymonds.

"I would take Wade and Diener over Boylan and Lee," noted John Dodds. "Wade is a better defensive player and shot blocker. Lee could rebound, but he didn't have to because he had Ellis and Whitehead around him."

"Butch was not as quick as Wade," noted Raymonds. "Butch was a better shooter. Butch couldn't jump like Wade. Butch was intelligent and knew the game very well. Wade has more freedom to do things on the court. I've seen Wade take over games."

"Whitehead and Ellis, the way they were playing in the '77 Final Four, would have been a tough match-up for Jackson and Merritt," Dodds noted, "because Whitehead was 6'10". Both teams were good rebounding teams, and both were good free-throw shooting teams. Those are the good characteristics of Final Four teams."

"Jimmy Boylan was a helluva shooter," stated Raymonds. "He never shot that much in our system. When Boylan was in high school, he was one of the leading scorers in the country. Boylan was a better defensive player than Diener. Diener, under this system, is a better offensive player. Boylan was limited by Al's system."

"Off the bench, Toone versus Novak would have been interesting," noted Dodds. "Both could have come off the bench and shot the long jumper. Novak and Toone were both weak defenders on the perimeter—Novak because he doesn't have the foot speed, Toone because he didn't have the will."

"There was another kid [Toone] who never knew his potential," Raymonds lamented.

"Bill Neary was the hatchet man for us," Raymonds continued. "He never wanted to shoot, never cared about scoring. But a helluva competitor. He was tough. Al really loved him. He was the enforcer. Neary was a defensive player, a rebounder. Townsend wasn't really a scorer, either. Townsend hustled. He did what he was told. Neary knew his role. He never took anything from anyone. Townsend was a role player, too." McGuire used to tell Neary to never shoot, unless he pulled down a rebound. Neary was also the only Wisconsin native who was a starter on the '77 champions. The 2003 squad had three: Jackson, Diener, and Merritt.

Dodds noted that comparisons between the backup guards (Gary Rosenberger and Karon Bradley) "would be favorable to Bradley."

"Both were outside shooters. Rosenberger was the better shooter, but Bradley is the more physical defender," Dodds noted.

When Dodds compared Ulice Payne Jr. (now president of the Milwaukee Brewers) to freshman Joe Chapman, he noted that "Ulice was a take-charge guy, while Chapman is a take-charges kind of guy."

Between Bo Ellis and Scott Merritt, Raymonds noted that Bo won the championship for Marquette. "Bo is why we won, no question. He could go inside, go outside. Big, long arms, good passer. Merritt is probably stronger physically. Whether he can shoot that much outside, Bo seemed to be a better outside shooter. I like Scott. That's another kid who has worked hard. This year he will blossom."

"It would be a great game if these two teams could play each other," said Raymonds. "It would depend on the rules."

When comparing McGuire and Crean, Raymonds noted that "Crean's more into basketball than Al was. Al was a gamer. In our days, if you stood up, people would yell at you to sit down.

"Al would do anything to take the pressure off the players. Al knew how to deal with officials. Crean talks to the officials, but it's different. It's more like talking on the street. But he is into the game. Al was more of a showman. He lived for the games."

During his 1999 interview with Dodds, McGuire insisted that for him basketball was never his life; it was a part of his life. "Basketball was a means to an end, not an end in itself." With Crean, the prototypical gym rat turned coach, he eats, drinks, and sleeps basketball so that he can learn and improve not just in the basketball sense, but as a coach. It is not unusual for Crean to call on coaching friends and pick their brains on strategy and motivation.

As voluble and animated as Crean is on the sidelines, he is not a coach who intentionally draws technical fouls during a game. In fact, Crean went through the entire 2002–03 season without drawing one technical foul. McGuire, who used the technical to his advantage, also worked the officials much differently; knowing how to use the language to get in an official's head during a game. That was his way of influencing the outcome, especially in a close contest.

After the team arrived in the Big Easy, the players received blue and gold beads as they alighted from the bus. They stayed at the Hotel Monteleone, on the fringe of the French Quarter. They were greeted at the hotel by so many well-wishers and fans, it was truly an extended Marquette family. A number of former players arrived, including Ron Curry, Tony Smith, and even the "Original Enforcer" himself, Hugh McMahon.

The players had their practice at Tulane University on Thursday. As part of the "championship every weekend" plan, Crean had the players wearing "Focus and Finish" T-shirts as a reminder of what they were in New Orleans to accomplish. It was after that practice that Dwyane Wade learned he was selected to the AP's First Team All-America squad, the first Marquette player so selected since Butch Lee in 1978.

That night, the players and coaches enjoyed the NCAA Tournament Dinner, where "One Shining Moment" composer David Barrett performed the Final Four signature song, featuring all of the "Moments" that had aired on CBS. Crean was so touched that he had a copy made. Afterward, the players had a taste of New Orleans on their night on the town before getting ready for their final championship weekend.

On Friday, April 4, it was back to business in preparing for Saturday afternoon's game against Kansas. It was the players' first trip back to the Superdome since the Tulane game in January. This was it. The basketball court was now in place, and they could begin to achieve what they had visualized since that November night when Crean showed them the photo of the Superdome. (Not to be outdone, Williams placed a photo of the Superdome in the lockers of his players before the season began.) The semifinal would also be the first time a Kansas team played at the Superdome. All of the players knew this was where Michael Jordan hit the winning shot in the 1982 championship to defeat Georgetown, and where Indiana's Keith Smart hit the game-winner to defeat Syracuse in 1987.

The Marquette team practice that day was not long compared to the typical Crean practices, but there was no time wasted. The team also practiced its game-winning shots as it had in Indianapolis, and ran off the floor after simulating such a shot to win the national championship.

Back in Wisconsin, the team was being sent well wishes by everyone, even in Madison, where a large blue-and-gold banner in the State Capitol blared, "GO MARQUETTE."

A bright sun rose above the French Quarter Saturday morning, April 5, on Final Four weekend. Breakfasters at the Hotel Monteleone looked at their *Times-Picayune* to see the four stars of the 2003 Final Four looking back at them from their sports section: T.J. Ford of Texas, Carmelo Anthony of Syracuse, Aaron Miles of Kansas, and Marquette's Wade.

As of Saturday morning, Marquette (27-5) was still a four-and-a-half-point underdog to the #2 seed Jayhawks (29-7), the same margin it had been all week leading up to the national semifinal. But Kansas began the season ranked No. 2 in the country and Marquette had been an underdog in every tournament game it played since the opening round against Holy Cross.

The War in Iraq was foremost in the minds of all Americans, including Tom Crean. The coach had received an e-mail from a soldier who was a Marquette grad. Crean told the *Times-Picayune*, "I think what basketball has turned out to be is a pretty good diversion for people to have something to look at. And that means a lot, it really does."

The war hit home even more so for Travis Diener, whose cousin, Derek, was stationed with a Patriot Missile group in the Mideast. "What they're doing over there is life and death," said Diener, who added that he kept a positive outlook. "I know the type of person he [Derek] is, and I have a very positive outlook on everything in life." The American flag on the front of each player's uniform served as a constant reminder of the war being waged half a world away.

On the basketball front, Marquette junior shooting guard Wade was quickly becoming known as "29-11-11" for his triple-double against Kentucky in the Midwest Regional Final, for which he was named Most Outstanding Player.

Crean said that he was impressed with Kansas' Nick Collison and his ability to slip screens and hit deep three-point shots. Collison returned the compliment in that day's stories, telling reporters that Marquette should be the favorite in the Final Four after the way it defeated Kentucky, the number one team in the nation. Diener told the *Times-Picayune*: "You really have to respect every team that makes the tournament, win or lose."

Crean was still enjoying the moment. It takes a little luck to get to the Final Four, and a little more to win the national championship. Crean was getting a lot of national publicity as a result of the Final Four run. He was the prototypical hot, young coach being mentioned for just about every major coaching opening in sight, including UCLA, North Carolina, Georgia, and any other slot that might open up. It was hard not to open a sports section and find some story or column touting his coaching genius. In fact, an unnamed Conference USA coach reportedly began referring to Crean as "Tommy Naismith," because the many stories made Crean sound like he had reinvented the game. There also may have been a twinge of jealousy since Crean was now the talk of the nation as well as the conference. Well, Crean looks like the old coach with the glasses and slicked-back hair. All he needs is the mustache. Even the *Chicago Tribune*'s Rick Morrissey had fun with Crean in his column, describing the young upstart as "The Coach Who Never Sits."

Marquette power forward Scott Merritt told the Times-Picayune, "We set our goals, just like everyone else. That's being national champions. I wouldn't have come to Marquette if I didn't think this was possible."

CBS' musical introduction for its Final Four broadcast that Saturday, which featured a French Quarter tribute to the four remaining teams, described Marquette as "wet behind the ears."

Marquette was the first Catholic school to make the Final Four since Seton Hall in 1989. Only two other non-BCS schools have made the Final Four: UMASS in 1996 and Utah in 1998.

With all of the questions surrounding the college basketball coaching carousel, including Pittsburgh, UCLA, and North Carolina, Crean said he did not let such talk become a distraction for his team. Crean was simply straight with his players, and that was all they needed to know.

Kansas coach Roy Williams had been prominently mentioned as a replacement for the recently-fired Matt Doherty at Carolina, whom Williams helped coach when he was an assistant to Dean Smith at Chapel Hill.

Williams, who had become friends with Crean at coaching clinics in recent years, noted that the hubbub over his rumored leaving for UNC had just the opposite effect. It kept him even more focused on the task at hand in the Final Four, which was his fourth while at Lawrence and his second straight.

Before their national semifinal game, CBS brought the two coaches together for a pre-game chat. It was obvious during the give and take that the coaches had a great mutual respect for each other. Williams noted that he genuinely liked and had a great deal of respect for Crean, and that the Marquette coach was a "coach's coach." "And that's the highest compliment I can give."

While Crean did not play college basketball, he did play ball at Mt. Pleasant High for Denny Kuiper, who came to New Orleans to support Crean and the Golden Eagles. Crean has always downplayed his high school basketball career by saying that he was an average player at best.

During its pregame show, CBS asked its "coaches roundtable," featuring Rick Majerus, Notre Dame's Mike Brey, and Oklahoma's Kelvin Sampson who they thought would be in the Monday night final and win the national championship. Majerus said that he was "going all the way with Marquette, baby," and that the Golden Eagles would defeat Syracuse behind "papal power." Brey favored the same two teams with a different result, and Sampson saw a Big 12 final between Texas and Kansas.

Marquette was not simply happy just to be in New Orleans. Diener reminded all who would listen to him that his team was not a Cinderella. "We've got the confidence and talent to win it," he told the *Times-Picayune*.

While experience in the Final Four is certainly a factor, Michigan State's Tom Izzo, who was brought on board by CBS as an analyst that weekend, said that he would rather have more experienced players than an experienced coach. Izzo should know, he has taken three teams to the Final Four. "And it is easier the second time around."

As the team bus arrived at the Superdome, the Marquette players alighted wearing their Walkman headphones. When CBS' Armen Keteyian caught up with Wade, he asked him how big a role Wade would have to play in the game. Wade deflected the question and stated that the team would just have to continue to play "Marquette basketball" and play tough defense.

When asked how to stop Wade, Kansas' Keith Langford said that you have to "throw out the scouting report" when trying to play him. Williams told Bonnie Bernstein that the Jayhawks would go with a one-on-one defense to try to stop him. Williams added that "Marquette has probably played the best basketball in the country over the last two weeks," and that he had not shown any tape of the Marquette-Kentucky game to his players.

Students, alums, young and old alike, from classes recent and distant, came to the Big Easy for the conclusion of the Big Dance, as did other fans who traveled from Milwaukee, including bandwagon jumpers. They were welcome, too.

Jerry DeBoer of Franklin, Wisconsin, became a Marquette fan during the team's breakout performance in the Great Alaska Shootout. "I was willing to jump on," DeBoer said unapologetically. "I didn't follow that [1977 team]." However, DeBoer was impressed with Al McGuire, especially his "speaking in metaphors, his quality insight. He tended to bring more depth to his pronouncements," noted DeBoer, who was graduated from Viterboo College in LaCrosse.

Also in New Orleans was Walter Affable, 25, of Chicago, a 1999 graduate who was born in 1977. Wearing a Dwyane Wade No. 3 jersey, Affable drove to New Orleans with two other Marquette alums. It was his first Final Four.

"I knew a little about it [the '77 championship]. I was more familiar with Al McGuire as a commentator. He was an eloquent man. With a unique commentary. He made it [analysis] almost like an art form. Tom Crean shows so many of the same qualities as Al McGuire. It's infectious," Affable added.

It all seemed so right for Marquette at the Final Four. A Catholic school named for a Jesuit French missionary (Pere Jacques Marquette), with the team staying in the French Quarter.

A wave of gold swept through New Orleans and Bourbon Street from the time the players arrived from Milwaukee on Wednesday evening.

"There were more Marquette fans in New Orleans than any of the other three schools," remarked Jim Ganzer, whose brother, Mike (a.k.a. "Gato 78"), added that, "Tom Crean is in control of and the ringleader of Al's Circus."

Even with all of the hubbub and distractions surrounding the Final Four, Crean managed to find some quality time with his family before the big game. He went swimming at the hotel pool with Megan and Riley before heading over to the Louisiana Superdome.

On Saturday afternoon, as a cast of thousands of Marquette fans, students, and alums crowded a ballroom at the Hyatt Hotel, a sea of gold caps, T-shirts, and bandanas trimmed with blue, were everywhere. The excitement and enthusiasm was palpable as the crowds swelled before the pre-game reception began in the ballroom.

Students and alums representing every era of Marquette basketball—Hilltoppers, Golden Avalanche, Warriors, and Golden Eagles—whatever the team happened to be called at the time—were all represented as one—WE ARE MARQUETTE! The occasional chants resounded throughout the ballroom, which was ringed with blue and gold balloons in horseshoe shapes.

At 2:15 p.m., Tom Pipines, sports director of WITI-TV, Channel 6 in Milwaukee, took the stage to rev up the crowd for a televised tease of its 10 p.m. newscast. The crowd responded to the prompting with chants ranging from WE ARE MARQUETTE to GO WARRIORS!

Donning gold T-shirts and the gold caps distributed at Al's Day, on January 25 at the Bradley Center, the extended Marquette family geared up for the upcoming National Semifinal, which was just under three hours away, with tip-off scheduled for 5:07 p.m.

The optimism and good feelings that filled the ballroom were infectious. Like spring training in baseball, each team in the Final Four believes it has a chance to win it all, even though each team travels a different road to the Final Four.

Music blared from the loudspeakers and videotaped highlights from the season just past and tournament games made the players seem larger than life.

At 2:20 p.m., the revelry was interrupted for the singing of "God Bless America," in honor of the troops fighting in Iraq.

Eileen Kane, a 1996 alumna from Chicago, when asked what she knew about Al McGuire's Final Four team in 1977, said, "I didn't know much about his teams, just that he was a class act."

"My dad idolized the guy," said fellow '96 alum Brian Roche. "We grew up on Marquette basketball. The difference between Coach McGuire and Coach Crean is that one is a legend and the other is a legend-in-the-making. Tom Crean is the hottest thing going."

When some of the alums were asked what they thought was a turning-point game during the season, the Feb. 27 contest at Louisville was at the top of the list.

Peter Pedraza, also a '96 alum, recalled, "The Louisville game was the turning point. It must have been a helluva halftime. We also went to Minnesota last weekend. The Kentucky game was dream-like. Is this happening?" All three alums are regulars at Halligan's Bar in Chicago, which shows the games during the season. "Positive" Pete Pedraza predicted that Marquette "was going to win it all."

Kane added: "I don't think anyone would be here if they didn't think we could do it."

Even with the great record Crean had established in his first four years, former Coach Hank Raymonds still had the best first four year win-loss record of ANY Marquette coach (McGuire and Crean included). Raymonds' four-year mark was 84-31, while Crean's was 83-41.

Marquette alumni staff handed out gold buttons and placards that read: "WE ARE MARQUETTE," in addition to the blue and gold lucky beads that alums, students, and friends of the program were wearing with pride. The only thing that Marquette backers really had to complain about was the official NCAA sanctioned memorabilia, especially the hats which were adorned with a single navy "M" instead of the traditional "MU" logo. "If you haven't been there, they don't know," noted Dodds, referring to the fact that Marquette's basketball team had been off the national radar for so long, the NCAA merchandising people did not know what the school logo looked like.

The pre-game reception and rally revved up the fans to a fever pitch before the main event at the Louisiana Superdome, just across the street from the Hyatt. Suffice it to say that all were in full throat well before tip-off. It sounded like what everyone could expect to hear in the cavernous arena, where some great college basketball Final Fours have been held, including those in 1982, 1987, and 1993.

A little less than two hours before game time, a cool breeze began to waft down Poydras Street, where the Superdome is located. Before the weekend, Crean had telephoned Dallas Cowboys' coach Bill Parcells asking if he would talk to the team before their game against the Jayhawks. Parcells respectfully declined, but told Crean that the team would not have to play its best game to win, but its smartest game.

During his pep talk to the team before they went out onto the court, Crean stood before the chalkboard, which featured the main points the team needed to focus on for the game. Crean delivered his talk in a rapid-fire monologue. It was hard to tell if he was more nervous because of the CBS cameras recording the session or because of the game.

He emphasized that all of the Marquette players would have to sprint back on defense and beat the Kansas players down the floor, winning the battle of the boards and getting to the free-throw line. "When you've had 25 attempts or more from the line, you've won," Crean reminded them.

"There's not a doubt we're gonna get pressed today, whether it's in the half court, when it comes to full court pressure or when it comes to token pressure. We gotta handle it to score and attack it to score.

"Kansas is by far the best passing team we've played all year. We've gotta take away the high-low. We've gotta take away the fast-break passing.

"We've gotta win the hidden points. And that's what we've been doing the entire tournament," continued Crean, who praised all of the things the team had accomplished up to that point.

"We've been winning coming out of time outs. We've been winning the baseline out of bounds. We've been winning the sideline out of bounds. We've been getting to loose balls. The four charges we drew last week, that has to turn into six or seven this week. It definitely can. It definitely can.

"All the keys are here. We continue to do what we gotta do in transition. Alright, we continue what we gotta do, with attacking the rim. And everything else will care of itself. The team that plays the hardest, the team that plays the smartest is the team that is going to win the game. But we gotta make sure these things come forth for us."

After the talk, Crean then showed the players every "One Shining Moment" that CBS has aired after its championship game telecasts. Before the team went out to the court, Crean showed the Golden Eagles just one cap: a Final Four cap. "This is the hat you have earned the right to wear," he reminded them.

The wave of gold moving down Poydras was interspersed with specks of blue and red, orange, and burnt orange, of the fans representing Kansas, Syracuse, and Texas, respectively, the other three Final Four entrants. But that sea of gold overwhelmed all.

One of the first omens that this was going to be a good night for Marquette was when St. John's, McGuire's alma mater, won the NIT in New York Friday night. This is Al's party and he wanted Marquette to be dancin' on Bourbon Street.

It seemed as if McGuire had all the planets aligned just right and the dancing lights moving just right for Marquette's One Shining Moment.

A second good omen occurred an hour before tip-off, as a soft rain began to fall upon New Orleans which soon turned into a downpour. The Marquette faithful were starting to think that a rainy night in New Orleans might be a good sign, 26 years after a rainy night in Georgia.

Fans were hoping that these omens would somehow negate the *Sports Illustrated* jinx. Having Wade on the cover, as he had been on the April 7 issue, caused concern among those in Marquette Nation.

Marquette students, clad in their gold T-shirts and jeans, marched through the rain to the Superdome, oblivious to the stormy conditions. None of the students seemed to be too worried about getting drenched, not on this night.

Taxicabs were few and far between before the game. Traffic was tied up all the way to the Superdome, where the sign, "THE ROAD ENDS HERE," may have been the worst omen of all.

In Milwaukee, a large white tent had been set up near the Marquette Memorial Union for students to watch the game. There were also alumni parties in and around the Union.

"The first 10 minutes and preceding it in the Union, there was a palpable level of excitement and anticipation for the game," said Dan Kelly, who was also on campus the night of the '77 championship. "People were so up, so lit, believing that their alma mater was marching to destiny."

At 4:45 p.m., waves of gold could be seen in the lower levels and upper reaches of the Superdome. The chants of WE ARE MARQUETTE reverberated throughout the cavernous saucer of a stadium, where 54,432 gathered for the first semifinal. The second would feature the remaining #1 seed Texas and #3 seed Syracuse.

At 4:50 p.m., the Marquette Band played "Great Balls of Fire." Marquette fans were much louder than their Kansas, Texas, and Syracuse counterparts. In a few sections of the Superdome, large swatches of gold could be seen. The colors of the other schools seemed indistinguishable.

As the Marquette players went through their paces, they seemed relaxed. When the Jayhawks came onto the floor, it was the Kansas fans' turn to roar for their team. And they let loose. Roy Williams sat relaxed on the bench. As he stole a look at the cheering Jayhawks fans, he allowed himself a knowing, confident smile.

At 4:57 p.m., the Marquette band belted out "Ring Out Ahoya." Not long after that, the CBS pre-game show ended, and Greg Gumbel and analysts Clark Kellogg and Michigan State coach Tom Izzo, found seats away from the hurriedly disassembled set.

At 5 p.m., the Marquette cheerleaders ran onto the floor with the school flag held aloft, bringing the players onto the court. A roar went up from Marquette Nation. The players looked relaxed as they took easy lay-ups and jump shots. The Kansas players circled around the Marquette players to begin their paces.

At courtside, Billy Packer and Jim Nantz finished their pre-game prep for the CBS telecast of the semifinals. His "Packer Points" talked about the possibility that Dwyane Wade could be the Danny Manning of the Final Four. He talked about how important it was for Marquette to get back on transition defense to keep Kansas from getting fast-points. Packer pointed out the matchup between Rob Jackson and Jeff Graves, and that if Graves was in foul trouble early, it could hurt Kansas. "Jackson will give Graves all he can handle," warned Packer.

The bands posed on opposite sides of the basketball court, dueling musicians doing their best to rev up their respective student sections.

At 5:04 p.m., the buzzer sounded in the Superdome, as the teams prepared for the introductions.

Marquette's starters all year—Todd Townsend, Scott Merritt, Robert Jackson, Dwyane Wade, and Travis Diener—were introduced for their very first Final Four. The Marquette band began to play "Ring Out Ahoya." At courtside were Steve "The Homer" True and George Thompson, sharing a laugh before the game.

The last time that a Marquette team had played Kansas in the NCAA Tournament was in the National Semifinals in 1974. Marquette won that game 64-51.

At 5:10 p.m., Kansas won the tip. The Jayhawks quickly raced down court and guard Aaron Miles hit a three-pointer to start the scoring. Kansas wasted no time. Then it confronted Marquette with a tough man-to-man defense, forcing Diener into a turnover.

This was not the tempo Marquette wanted. The Jayhawks were ready to run, the Golden Eagles were not. It resembled the beginning of Marquette's game against Kentucky. It would be a long night.

After the Jayhawks went up 7-2, Marquette began to pick up the slack a little and start to run its offense. After a Wade basket and a Diener three-pointer, Kansas quickly got down court for a layup. 9-7 Kansas. Marquette tied it, then Aaron Miles was fouled on a basket and hit the free throw to put Kansas ahead, 12-9.

Marquette was not getting back quickly enough in its transition defense.

Back in Milwaukee, "There was a little shock and disbelief in the first half," Kelly said. "People were looking around and shaking their heads, wondering how this could be happening, especially after what they did to Kentucky."

It seemed that Kansas gave a whole new meaning to the military phrase that had gained popularity at the time, "shock and awe."

As the time-out ended, the Marquette Band began exhorting the Golden Eagle fans in WE ARE MARQUETTE.

After Wade made two free throws, the game was tied at 12, which helped inspire the team's defense. But everything after that seemed like a blur. For every basket Marquette scored, it seemed that Kansas scored two. That was how quickly the Jayhawks went down the floor. The following sequence seemed to sum up the first half: Langford layup. Novak missed three. Hinrich answers with a three. Wade drives, gets fouled. Missed one of two free throws. Kansas three-pointer. Marquette misses shot and has ball stolen. Hinrich hits a three. Marquette time-out. Kansas up 23-14. Marquette would score just 16 more points the rest of the half.

"After 12-12, it was almost a whisper," said Steve True.

It seemed as if Marquette was standing still. Kansas players were beating Marquette down the floor on almost every possession. Apart from its hot shooting, Kansas was a step faster and Marquette could not get its shots to fall. Even the gimmes two feet from the basket were bouncing out. The Golden Eagles shot 31 percent from the field and 18.8 percent from three-point range (3 of 16). Kansas shot 53 percent from the field. The last team to shoot that well against Marquette was Notre Dame, way back in December.

McGuire used to say that in the NCAA Tournament, a team will have one bad shooting night. This happened to be Marquette's bad shooting night. What was most puzzling was that the team had been shooting the lights out in domed stadiums—the RCA Dome and the Metrodome. But the Superdome was not the charm for Marquette.

As the lead expanded for Kansas, Billy Packer noted that Wade as an All-America had to take charge for Marquette to try to bring them back. But it was too late. In the earlier tournament games when one Golden Eagle or the other was not hitting, someone else would step up. This night, no one was hitting.

Halftime: Kansas 59, Marquette 30. Before the CBS crew readied its set for the halftime show, a glum Tom Izzo sat watching, slumped in his chair. It was obvious how badly he felt for his former assistant. It was obviously tough for Izzo to watch.

"The clock seemed to take forever in the second half," said True.

In Milwaukee, "there was a sense of resignation," Kelly noted. "Coupled with a sense, albeit meek, of hope. It was gonna be a tremendous mountain to climb, but they had seen comebacks before and beat teams they weren't supposed to beat during the tournament and the season."

As if that were not tough enough, Crean's mother, Marjorie, was taken to the hospital in the second half, unbeknownst to her son. She felt numbness and was taken to a local hospital where she was diagnosed with a stroke.

"Shortly into the second half, the tone shifted to complete resignation. Many people were not even paying attention to the game," said Kelly of the Milwaukee alums, who were taking the time to catch up with "people we hadn't seen in 20 years. After it was over, there did not seem to be a lot of bitterness, but instead a lot of gratitude for where the team had ended up that season. After all, no one expected the team to be in the Final Four."

Insult was added to injury late in the game when the eerie strains of "Rock Chalk, Jayhawk" undulated throughout the Superdome.

Losing 94-61 was tough, as tough as the North Carolina game two years earlier. But like that game, this Final Four was a measuring stick, and it showed the team what it takes to win a Final Four and a national championship. In 1990, Duke lost the national championship to UNLV by 30 points, and went on to win the next two national championships.

Wade scored 19 points, followed by Jackson's 15 and Merritt's 12. Diener scored only five points on 1 of 11 shooting and had eight turnovers. Clearly, he was not 100 percent, physically. The shin splints certainly were a problem. One of the few bright spots was that Tony Gries, Chris Grimm, and Jared Sichting did get a chance to play in the Final Four.

"Losses like that are not good ones to do," said True. "How many years in a row would you go to the Final Four if you knew you were going to lose by 30? Two, but not three."

In the postgame press conference, Diener and Wade said they were "extremely disappointed" in the outcome and their play. But they pointed out that while this Final Four disappointment would stay with them forever, that their great season and incredible run to the Final Four would also stay with them forever. When it was Crean's turn at the podium, he noted that the team just could not get any runs put together at all. He also noted that there was a definite lack of communication by the players on the defensive end. The loss was a tough comeuppance.

Izzo came over to the Hotel Monteleone to talk to Crean after the game. As he entered the lobby, he told a visitor that his Spartans had to go through the same kind of tough loss in the tournament before they could take that next step to winning a national championship. "They'll get there," Izzo promised.

Marjorie Crean was resting comfortably in a New Orleans hospital after the game, and after a brief recovery was able to return to the Midwest with the rest of the family.

After the game, the atmosphere at what was to be the post-game celebration was somber. It was a tough night for Marquette, especially on the national stage of the Final Four.

The Marquette players and coaches came back to the Hyatt, where earlier in the day they had enjoyed a rousing send-off, greeted by some 1,000 fans. "The players were visibly shaken," recalled Ganzer. "They felt like they had let the fans down."

A large color photo in the *Chicago Sun-Times* the next morning, showing a dismissive Roy Williams looking down at a supine Wade, said it all: Marquette had fallen and it could not get up. In the *Milwaukee Journal*

Sentinel, the headline was "That's All She Wrote," and in the *Chicago Tri-bune,* "Jayhawk Cakewalk."

The sun shone brightly on the French Quarter Sunday morning. It was a new day, with all the hope of bigger and better things to come.

As morning turned into afternoon, the sea of gold that so dominated the Big Easy had dissipated some. Some of the Marquette players were walking around the shops, picking out some memorabilia to take home from their Big Dance in the Big Easy.

Later that afternoon, friends of the Marquette program returned to the Hotel Monteleone to celebrate the season. Alums, young and old alike, reminisced about the successful season and exciting tournament, and how the best was yet to come. It was a great journey with great expectations.

Marquette stayed in New Orleans to watch Syracuse defeat Kansas for the national championship. Crean wanted the players to take in the entire Final Four experience and see what it took to win a national title.

"Marquette lost to Kansas," noted Fedders, "but you have to think that those other games leading up to it were great wins. It was an amazing feat, those four games in the NCAA Tournament. To beat those four teams," and to have beaten five conference champions overall.

Marquette's March to Madness may have ended in New Orleans, but one game does not define a season, regardless of how big the stage is. The crucible of the Final Four will serve to mold this young group for future trips and future national championships. They had a taste of the honey, and now they want more. The chip on their shoulders is now firmly in place. Crean could not come up with a more powerful motivational tool than the result of this game. The Golden Eagles won almost as many NCAA Tournament games (4) during its run as the basketball program had won total since the last title in 1977 (5).

To paraphrase Bo Ellis after McGuire's Warriors lost the 1974 national championship to North Carolina State: "We'll be back. Not here, but somewhere else in a championship game. This was the wrong place and the wrong time, but we'll be back." ∎

EPILOGUE

After the Final Four, there was quite a bit of speculation about the futures of both Crean and Wade.

Crean was considered the hottest young basketball coach in America after the tournament. He had polished his resume nicely with the Clair Bee Award.

The media's domino theory did not quite work as it was laid out in the weeks that followed the NCAA Championship game.

When Roy Williams left Kansas to take over the North Carolina program from the fired Matt Doherty, it was speculated that Illinois coach Bill Self would take over for Williams, leaving the Illini job open for Crean.

In the meantime, the Pittsburgh job opened up when Ben Howland finally did jump and take the UCLA job, thus fueling more speculation for Crean. Another opening for Crean's consideration.

Unbeknownst to most media, Marquette Athletic Director Bill Cords had already begun work on a contract extension for Crean prior to the Final Four. As is his nature, Cords did his work quietly, not seeking any media attention. When Crean returned to Milwaukee with his family, he spent time helping his mother rehabilitate from her stroke, in addition to his coaching duties.

As the dominos began to fall, Crean's name floated to the top of the wish list of Illini AD Ron Guenther. During the media circus that followed, Cords was reportedly not officially asked by Illinois for permission to talk to Crean.

Neither Crean nor Cords made any public pronouncements while the speculation percolated. Cords did say that Crean was all about relationships, and that was most important to him. Crean had committed to Marquette and Marquette had committed to him. He was also committed to the players and they to him. He rebuilt the basketball program and put his imprimatur on it. Crean embraced the McGuire legacy and built on it with the team and the newly built McGuire Center.

"Al and Tom put Marquette first and wear their loyalty on their sleeves," commented John Fedders. The way they talk about Marquette. The way Tom handled his contract extension. It's [Marquette] a good place to coach, and since there's no football program, they are kings. By being king, that loyalty is in the forefront in the way they both wear Marquette University."

Said Fran Fraschilla of ESPN: "Tom demands a lot, school, etc., and the players enjoy it. There's a magic about that."

As the speculation heated up, one Milwaukee-area newspaper declared that Crean going to Illinois was a done deal. The rumors grew to the point that Crean was said to be grooming his mentor, Ralph Willard of Holy Cross, to take over at Marquette once Crean signed with Illinois.

It grew more intense when assistants Dwayne Stephens and Darrin Horn left Marquette. Stephens returned to Michigan State to assist Izzo and Horn was hired as the head coach at Western Kentucky, his alma mater.

Adding more fuel to the fire was the uncertainty of the future of Conference USA, in the wake of the invitation of the Big East's Miami, Boston College, and Syracuse to join the ACC.

Crean, however, continued to work out his players in practices and prepare for more recruiting trips. He accompanied Robert Jackson to an NBA camp in Portsmouth, Virginia, and flew to Los Angeles with Wade for the Wooden Awards.

The class Crean was welcoming for the fall of 2003 included 6'8" James Matthews and 5'11" Brandon Bell, both of Michigan; 6'5" Dameon Mason of West Aurora, Illinois, one of the top players in that state; Carlton Christian, a 6'4" forward from Florida; and 6'9" center Marcus Jackson, who decided to transfer from Georgia. Recruiting guru Bob Gibbons tabbed the class #6 in the country, the first time a Marquette recruiting class had achieved top 10 status. But Crean, as he has the past four years, will develop this talent and mold a team.

The speculation heated up even more when it was announced that Crean was going to hold a press conference in the early evening of April 19, to make an announcement. At the Alumni Memorial Union, he announced that he had finalized a "more than generous" long-term contract extension to stay at Marquette.

During his announcement, Crean talked about some of the speculation and how the reported sources in some of the stories had never even talked to him. He mentioned that after he and the team returned from the Final Four, they went back to work, doing their jobs and preparing for next season.

Crean said that he had spent a good deal of time with his mother while she recuperated at their home in suburban Milwaukee. That brings up another similarity between Crean and McGuire: strong mother figures. Marjorie Crean and the late Winnie McGuire were both strong women who never feared a hard day's work. They were also strong in their personal beliefs and values.

There were a lot of surprised people, especially in Illinois, who felt that the Big Ten had more to offer than Marquette. Crean said in his statement that he and his family were happy in Milwaukee and that there was still unfinished business for his team. According to a Sportsline.com column written by Dan Wetzel, three days after Crean announced his contract extension, Crean believes he can win a national championship at Marquette.

"This is a statement that should ring loudly and true to recruits throughout the Midwest. Crean said no to the Big Ten; you can, too. Crean believes you can win the tourney at MU, and so should you. When Crean talks about catching a dream, he's dreaming right with you," said Wetzel.

Crean's decision was a breath of fresh air in the big money world of college sports. And along with the prestige of a Final Four, doors get opened to recruits. It was not long after Crean announced his contract extension, that Marquette and Arizona had agreed to a home-and-home series beginning next season in Tucson. That was followed later by the announcement that Marquette will play in Costa Rica in October. This has showed a renewed respect for the program by the elite of college basketball and that Crean and his program are once again becoming big time players.

Al McGuire made Marquette a destination job for coaches. Tom Crean confirmed that by returning the Golden Eagles to the Final Four and staying in Milwaukee. "The only thing I ever told coaches was to go to a school where you can get to the Final Four," McGuire told John Dodds in their 1999 interview. "You can't get to the Final Four from Vanderbilt, Davidson, Dartmouth or Northwestern."

The only downside Raymonds saw from the Final Four run is the heightened expectations for the team. "He [Crean] has recreated a monster. Fans won't be satisfied with just beating a team; they'll want the players to bury them."

In his contract announcement, Crean stated that he had a great deal of pride in the university, the basketball program, its players, as well as in the community and the state of Wisconsin. He had high praise for the players, and gave them credit for the success Marquette had enjoyed during the season, even though it ended in a tough loss. But Crean insisted that the "process," the journey, if you will, is really more important than the result of one game. And that is what he looks at when a practice is completed, when a game is over, and when a season is done: how much did we improve? How much did we get better?

Also, the McGuire Center was scheduled to open in the fall of 2003, a facility he had dedicated much time and effort to in the past three years.

Cords said the main reason he and Crean did not answer questions during the contract negotiation process was that they had nothing to report. Both men kept their counsel to themselves, and to their credit did not let anything about the process leak to the press. A great example of how to keep contract negotiations watertight. Nothing leaked.

Cords was quick to announce that there was no escape clause in the contract that would allow Crean to leave for Michigan State or Kentucky or any school. He also would not answer questions about the Illinois head-coaching job. He concluded by saying that it was a great time for Marquette University.

Crean filled the first of his open assistant positions by hiring Kyle Green of Northern Iowa. He filled the other position by bringing back Marquette legend, Bo Ellis, who had been fired as head coach at Chicago State after a tough four years. Ellis was then hit by tragedy in July when his daughter, Nikki, a former Marquette women's team assistant, died suddenly. Crean, class act that he is, waited until after the Ellis family took care of its arrangements before making the announcement. Ellis, the only Marquette player to ever play in two Final Fours, will be the keeper of the '77 flame and help his new charges stir the flame anew.

And Brian Wardle came full circle when he was hired as Marquette's director of basketball operations during the summer.

There was another tragedy in the Marquette family in June, when McGuire's "Black Swan," Bob Lackey, died of cancer at age 53.

While there was still uncertainty as to whether Wade would remain at Marquette for another year (he had two years of eligibility remaining), he continued to attend class and practice with his teammates, as if he were staying. What was most unusual about this most unusual of future NBA Lottery picks, was that he was continuing his school work when most players headed for the NBA drop classes before the draft. Not Wade. He even took his final exams.

In May, after Crean and Wade returned from the Wooden Awards in Los Angeles, Wade made his not-too-surprising announcement that he was turning professional. When he did announce, it was a tough day for Crean, who was a little choked up during the announcement. Crean's loyalty and attachment to his players is such that he finds it easier to talk about them than himself.

When Crean was asked during the press conference if Wade's No. 3 jersey was going to be retired, he said, "Yes, as soon as he gets his degree."

"In their loyalty to their kids, both Al and Tom see a superparental responsibility. Al was much more secretive," explained Fedders.

"Gary Rosenberger told me a story about when he was at school and had an apartment near the Old Gym. Al would always stop in and borrow a dollar from Gary. Gary kidded about it. I said to Gary, 'I don't know what was going on in your life at that time, but Al never did anything that was an accident. I'll bet he was worried about something that was going on in your life.'

"As I watch Tom, with the emotion he shared with Dwyane Wade's departure from Marquette, I recalled Al's talks with players' mothers. I sat in on a couple of kitchens when he talked to mothers. He would tell them about taking the kids uptown, getting an education, and raising their station in life. Tom Crean hasn't had that history, but I see the same dedication to his kids," concluded Fedders.

Wade was a finalist for several player-of-the-year awards, was the first Marquette player named consensus First Team All-America since Butch Lee, and, based on his incredible performances during the NCAA Tournament, he was ready for the next step in his playing career.

When Wade stood on the stage at Madison Square Garden with NBA Commissioner David Stern as the fifth pick in the draft by the Miami Heat, he set another record: Highest NBA draft pick from Marquette University. EVER.

Wade had come full circle that season. He started his regular season at Madison Square Garden, putting on a show against Villanova to kick off Marquette's magical season, and now he was taking the next giant step in his basketball career.

Marquette took a chance and gave Wade an opportunity. Wade brought Marquette as close to the promised land as it had been in over a generation. Neither he nor Marquette owed each other anything. Both he and Marquette were paid in full.

The basketball team traveled 7,452 miles on its magical journey to the Final Four this season. If a journey of 10,000 miles begins with one step, a journey of 7,452 miles begins with a slam dunk.

Al McGuire's journey to the '77 national championship validated his coaching career. The journey of the 2003 Marquette Golden Eagles validated their return to the elite of college basketball. ▪